ARNHEM

*British Battles Series*

# ARNHEM

## MAJOR-GENERAL R. E. URQUHART
### C.B., D.S.O.

**UNABRIDGED**

PAN BOOKS LTD : LONDON

First published 1958 by Cassell & Co. Ltd.
This edition published 1960 by Pan Books Ltd,
33 Tothill Street, London, S.W.1

ISBN 0 330 23273 8

2nd (Re-set) Printing 1972

© 1958 by Major-General R. E. Urquhart, CB, DSO

To all ranks who served in the
1st Airborne Division in September 1944
and their Comrades in Arms of the
1st Polish Parachute Brigade Group

Printed in Great Britain by
Cox & Wyman Ltd., London, Reading and Fakenham

# ILLUSTRATIONS
# IN PHOTOGRAVURE

# MAPS

# APPENDIXES

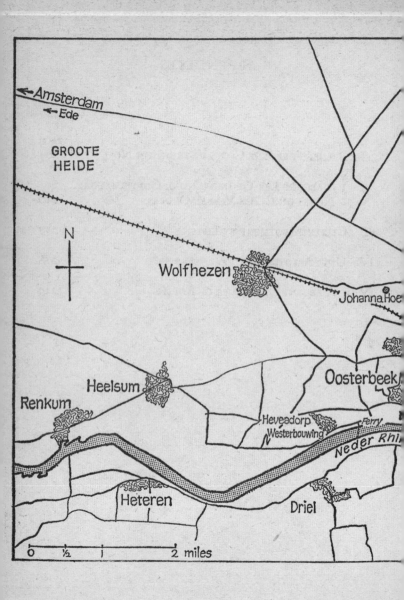

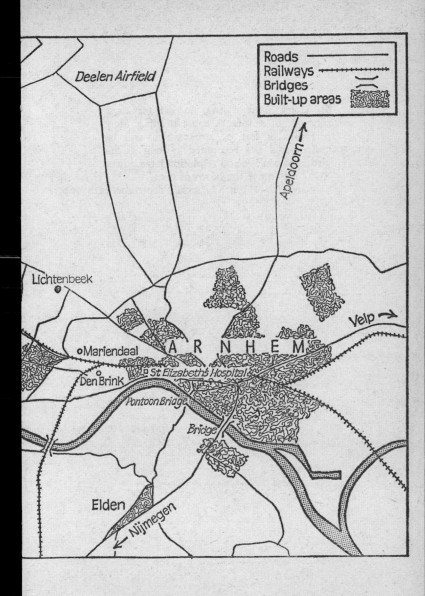

Roads ————
Railways +++++++
Bridges ⌣
Built-up areas

Deelen Airfield

Apeldoorn ↑

Lichtenbeek

Velp →

A R N H E M

Mariendaal

St Elizabeth5 Hospital

Den Brink

Pontoon Bridge

Bridge

Elden

Nijmegen ←

'In attack most daring, in defence most cunning, in endurance most steadfast, they performed a feat of arms which will be remembered and recounted as long as the virtues of courage and resolution have power to move the hearts of men.'

– *Winston Churchill*, September 28th, 1944

# PREFACE

This is the story of the 1st Airborne Division at Arnhem during the Operation 'Market Garden' which involved not only an airborne corps of three Divisions but also the bulk of the British 2nd Army in Europe. The 'Market' part of the operation covered the action of the Airborne troops and 'Garden' the ground operations which were designed to join up with them. Considerable attention has been focused on the action of my Division and sometimes it is too easily forgotten that the other two Airborne Divisions, the 82nd and the 101st which were American, also had tremendous battles in their own sectors.

'Market' was an airborne corps battle and the success or failure of the operation must be viewed as a whole.

In order to prevent the story of this action, which at times was very confused, from becoming merely a narrative of events in the style of an official history, it has been found impossible to give prominence to all, both units and individuals, who deserve mention for their part in this battle. Some are mentioned often but this does not mean that the performance of others, who are either not named at all or are very briefly dealt with, is undervalued. All units and all ranks played their part in this very intensive nine days and I wish it were possible to deal with them all equally in the text.

I would like to thank the many who have helped me in the preparation of this book by either lending their own personal accounts of the battle or allowing themselves to be interviewed.

I have to thank General Eisenhower, Field-Marshal Viscount Montgomery of Alamein and Lieutenant-General Sir Frederick Browning for allowing the reproduction of their letters to me in connexion with this action.

Finally I must acknowledge the help which Wilfred Greatorex has given me in the preparation of this book. Without him the account would never have been written.

His professional skill has been of the greatest assistance in the arrangement of the material and the stories of those days and it is to be hoped that the result is such as to make evident something of the spirit and fighting ability of the 1st Airborne Division.

R.E.U.

# CHAPTER ONE

WITH A grand sweep of the hand, my Corps commander, Boy Browning, drew a third large circle on the talc-covered map and, fixing me with his hard and direct gaze, said: 'Arnhem Bridge – and hold it.' The three circles represented the 'airborne carpet' along which Montgomery intended to roll the victorious 2nd Army from the Dutch–Belgian border all the way across Holland to the Zuider Zee ninety-nine miles away. It was nothing if not daring. Monty had two major objectives: to get troops over the formidable Rhine barrier, and to capture the Ruhr. Further, he planned by this powerful stroke to cut off the escape route of the Germans still in western Holland, some of whom were responsible for the V2 attacks on England; to outflank the Reich's West Wall, and to give the Allies a springboard for a rapid drive across the north German plain.

As deputy to the American commander of the Allied Airborne Army, General Lewis Brereton, Browning was responsible for ground operations. As he elaborated on the plan, I glanced at the two American generals sitting alongside me and wondered if they were as surprised as I was at the boldness of the whole conception – coming as it did from the usually cautious Monty. Major-General Max Taylor and his 101st US Airborne Division were responsible for the stretch of carpet which included the river crossings between Eindhoven and Grave, and Jim Gavin and his 82nd US Airborne Division for the middle length and the crossings of the River Maas at Grave and the Waal at Nijmegen. It occurred to me that it was either a compliment to the efficiency of my own 1st Airborne Division that we had been given the farthest bit of carpet or an instance of safety-first diplomacy in view of the fact that the idea was Monty's and the operation British. If I had known all that had transpired between the birth of the idea in Monty's agile mind and its acceptance by SHAEF, I might well have taken the latter view. For Eisenhower, as Supreme Commander, did not see eye to eye with Monty

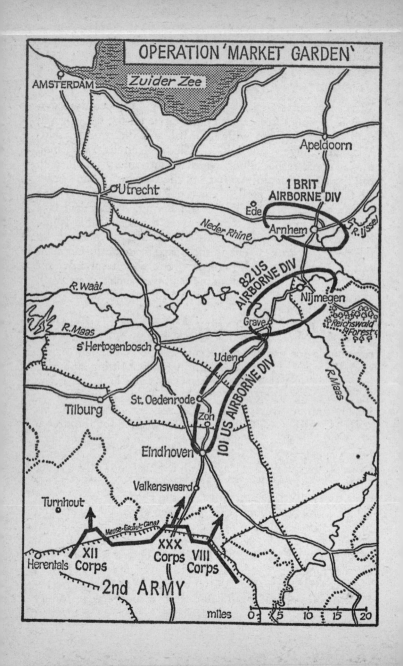

about the immediate shape of operations against the now battered Germans. While Eisenhower favoured an advance along a broad front, taking advantage of all lines of attack, Monty saw an opportunity for 'one really powerful and full-blooded thrust' in the north. As Eisenhower was later to write: 'There was still a considerable reserve in the middle of the enemy country and I knew that any pencil-like thrust into the heart of Germany such as he proposed would meet nothing but certain destruction.' This fundamental disagreement blew up when they met in Eisenhower's aircraft on Brussels airfield on the afternoon of September 10th, 1944.

Monty, living up to his reputation for pushing his own point of view, prevailed on Ike to allow him to use the airborne force to seize the crossings over the Maas, the Waal and the Neder Rhine. In acceding to Monty's plan, however, Eisenhower was not going contrary to his own views. Whereas Monty visualized the operation as a vital knockout punch, Ike merely saw it as an extension of his broad front plan. And even when he had set the ball rolling, Monty found that Ike had not given him priority over other operations farther south. With such powerful American generals as Bradley and Patton likely to be affected by any such decision, this was not surprising.

Thus, in its early stages, Operation 'Market Garden' was not the best example of Anglo-American accord.

It was not unreasonable that the 1st Airborne Division was given the sharp end. Long after the war, I learned that an American official account of the battle states that the 101st US Airborne Division was first assigned Arnhem and that the 1st Airborne Division then requested a switch because of our familiarity with the terrain through planning an earlier operation. While it is certainly true that we had studied the area for Operation 'Comet', in which we had the hazardous task of doing exactly what the entire Corps was about to do in 'Market Garden', I knew of no switch and definitely requested none. Browning made no such request on our behalf.

As far as I was concerned, Arnhem was our task from the start. Nevertheless I cannot help feeling that if one of the

American divisions had been in our place, the effect on international relations would have been most serious. The circumstances which were to prevent the British 2nd Army from joining up with the airborne force north of the Neder Rhine would not have been understood at all if the stranded force had been American. Every possible accusation would have been levelled at the 2nd Army for its failure to appear at the right time and place. It would have produced a most unfortunate influence on relations between our two countries and would not easily have been forgotten.

Although he appeared so confident at our briefing in his sparsely furnished room in the elegant pillared clubhouse at Moor Park, Browning himself harboured some reservations about the practicability of the whole thing. When he had been given his orders in Monty's caravan the day before, he asked how long we would be required to hold the Arnhem Bridge.

'Two days,' said Monty briskly. 'They'll be up with you then.'

'We can hold it for four,' Browning replied. 'But I think we might be going a bridge too far.' He was troubled about the distance that the 2nd Army would have to cover before it reached Arnhem. The main drive would come from Brian Horrocks' XXX Corps, with VIII and XII Corps on its flanks. The start line was the bridgehead over the Meuse-Escaut Canal south of Eindhoven.

Already there were ominous creaks coming from Monty's overstrained supply lines. Antwerp was still not open for shipping and he was relying on long-distance road convoys from France. Monty saw as clearly as anyone the logistic snags, and the further demands on his transport caused by the need to bring up VIII Corps caused him to signal Eisenhower on Monday September 11th that he would not attack before September 23rd. As a direct result of this representation he was promised a massive supply programme by the Americans, by road and air – a thousand tons a day until October 1st. Thus placated, he set forward D-Day to September 17th.

Before I went off to my caravan to make my plan, Browning informed me that he had persuaded the RAF to agree to a daylight operation and that, because of the limited number

16

of aircraft available, we would have to go in three lifts. Throughout the war, airborne forces were bedevilled by a chronic shortage of aircraft. It was a commander's job to try to get as many tugs and gliders for his men as he could, without too much consideration for the other fellow's demands, but in this case the situation was complicated because we were depending so much on the Americans for air transport – and our companion divisions in the operation were both American: the RAF alone could hardly have got half the division off the ground. Nevertheless, I began to prod Browning and his staff regularly for more and more aircraft. Once, when I suggested that I could do with forty more planes in order to satisfy my ground plan and Browning was pessimistic about my getting even a proportion of them, I raised the telling fact that the two American divisions were doing somewhat better. He assured me that this was due not to any high-level American pressure but solely to the natural order of priorities. 'It's got to be bottom to top,' he said, 'otherwise you'd stand the chance of being massacred.' As things were working out, Max Taylor and the 101st would go in at full strength and it was important to try to put down as many of Jim Gavin's 82nd as possible in one lift, though in the event Gavin had to make do with two lifts.

My plan had to be tailored to fit three lifts.

I had ten squadrons of 38 Group and six squadrons of 46 Group to take in the glider element, and the 9th US Troop Carrier Command was laying on the Dakotas for the parachutists. I reckoned I would need about 130 aircraft for each parachute brigade. My division consisted of the 1st and 4th Parachute Brigades and the 1st Airlanding Brigade, which was gliderborne. In addition, we had the normal number of divisional troops. And for this operation I had under command the 1st Polish Independent Parachute Brigade Group under Major-General Sosabowski. It had a small glider element.

The plan had to be produced quickly in order that it could be tied in with the American efforts at Grave and Nijmegen and also to allow time for it to be developed or amended in accordance with the RAF's wishes. I also had to allow for the movement of men from their stations to the airfields, for the production of up-to-date photographs, for briefings and for the loading of aircraft and gliders.

When Comet had been cancelled earlier that Sunday, September 10th, some of my staff officers, including Charles Mackenzie, my chief staff officer, had gone boating on the Thames; Boy Wilson, a middle-aged but virile parachutist of great experience who commanded the Independent Company, and others, had nipped off home to see their families. The boating party was rounded up and Wilson just had time to eat a domestic lunch before returning in his jeep. Wilson, who was to lead the force that would mark out the dropping and landing zones, was soon occupied studying the latest air photographs of the area. Mackenzie was busy with the air staff and during the evening I talked things over with my chief intelligence officer, Hugh Maguire, and Robert Loder-Symonds, the chief gunner.

I should have liked to put in troops on both sides of the river and as close as possible to the main bridge. This was unacceptable to the RAF, however, because of the flak barrage which bomber crews on their nightly visits to the Ruhr reported as extremely heavy in the Arnhem area. It was also considered that the tug aircraft, in turning away after releasing their gliders in this area, would either have run straight into the flak over Deelen airfield some seven miles to the north or into a mix-up with the aircraft involved in the Nijmegen airlift. Furthermore, the intelligence experts regarded the low-lying polderland south of the bridge as unsuitable for both gliders and parachutists. These limitations were closely examined but the RAF had already conceded as much as they were ever likely to concede in agreeing to a daylight operation. An airborne operation remains the airmen's responsibility until such time as the troops are put on the ground. The airmen had the final say, and we knew it.

Many experienced parachutists would have been quite prepared to have been dropped in the polder even though it was reported to be boggy, and in fact some of them would have been quite happy to have landed on the town itself and risked physical injury.

The influence of the flak picture on the RAF ruled out any

possibility of putting in even a small *coup-de-main* force in the vicinity of the bridge. From the maps and aerial photographs spread out before me in the caravan I saw that the only practical alternative for a force of any size was the open country west-north-west of Arnhem. There were broad expanses of flat ground some 250 feet above sea level and lying between belts of screening woodland. I checked the distances to the target and found that this ground was between six and eight miles away – a formidable distance for, as we had very little transport, the majority of the troops would have to cover the ground on foot. It had certain advantages: the ground would be firm and also ideal for quick re-grouping. I checked once more and could see no reasonable alternative. I now began to mark and allocate the likely dropping zones and landing areas.

The main handicap of having to go in three separate lifts was that not only had I to get enough men down in the first lift to seize the main bridge deep in the town but also to hold the dropping zones and landing areas for the succeeding lifts. This meant that the effective offensive strength of the division in the first day against the main objective was reduced to one parachute brigade.

I had no choice.

The planning of the operation was not helped by the scanty intelligence that was coming our way. I knew extremely little of what was going on in and around Arnhem and my intelligence staff were scratching around for morsels of information. I knew that what information we had received from across the Channel was bound to be out of date: it had filtered through various offices in the 2nd Army and our own corps before it reached us. In the division there was a certain reserve about the optimistic reports coming through from 21st Army Group concerning the opposition we were likely to meet. Obviously we would have liked a more recent intelligence picture, but we were subordinate to corps in such matters. Browning himself told me that we were not likely to encounter anything more than a German brigade group supported by a few tanks. Already, however, Dutch resistance reports had been noted to the effect that 'battered panzer

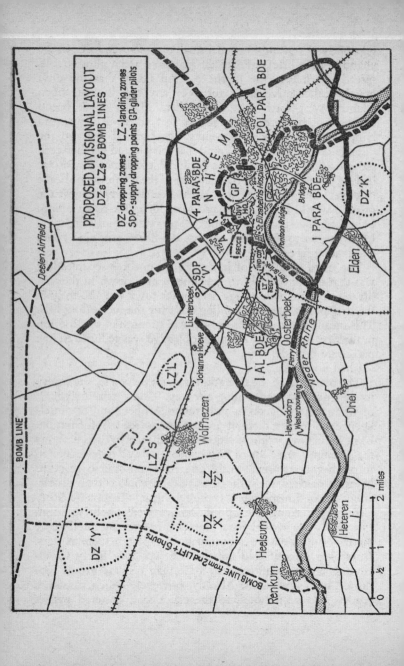

PROPOSED DIVISIONAL LAYOUT
DZs LZs & BOMB LINES

DZ=dropping zones   LZ=landing zones
SDP=supply dropping points  GP=glider pilots

BOMB LINE

Deelen Airfield

DZ "Y"

LZ "S"

DZ "X"

LZ "Z"

LZ "L"

Wolfhezen

Johanna Hoeve

Lichterbeek

SDP "V"

4 PARA BDE

A R N H E M

GP

DIV
HQ

RECCE

St. Elizabeth's Hospital

1 POL PARA BDE

DZ "K"

Bridge

Pontoon Bridge

Der Brink

2nd Bn

LT
REGT

1 AL BDE

Oosterbeek

Heveadorp

Westerbouwing

Ferry

Elden

1 PARA BDE

BOMB LINE from 2nd LIFT + 6 hours

Renkum

Heelsum

Neder Rhine

Driel

Heteren

2 miles

0   ½   1

remnants have been sent to Holland to refit', and Eindhoven and Nijmegen were mentioned as the reception areas. And during the week an intelligence officer at SHAEF, poring over reports and maps, came to the conclusion that these panzer formations were the 9th and possibly the 10th SS Panzer Divisions. It was likely that they were being re-equipped with new tanks from a depot in the area of Cleves, a few miles over the German border from Nijmegen and Arnhem. The SHAEF officer's opinion was not shared by others and, even as our preparations continued, 21st Army Group Intelligence were making it plain that they didn't see eye to eye with SHAEF over the panzer divisions. Nothing was being allowed to mar the optimism prevailing across the Channel. We all shared it to a certain degree, and this was particularly the case in our own Airborne Corps. On September 13th, four days before the attack, corps blithely passed on the information that the Germans in Holland had few infantry reserves and a total armoured strength of not more than fifty to a hundred tanks. And even if there was some evidence that the Germans were reinforcing their river lines near Arnhem and Nijmegen, the soldiers manning these defences were said to be few and 'of low medical category'.

I had no illusions about the Germans folding up at the first blow. I counted on the likelihood that his retaliation would get fiercer by the hour. He would be steadily reinforced whereas we would not be at full strength until well into the third day. He would also have whatever advantages were going in the way of heavy weapons: it is one of the calculated risks of all airborne operations that the assault goes in without the support of heavy weapons, and my only resources in this respect was the Light Regiment with its 75-mm guns firing a comparatively light shell. I marked the landing and dropping zones, three of them north of the Arnhem–Utrecht railway line which I designated L, S and Y, and two others south of the railway and north of Heelsum village – X and Z. Then I marked an area where the Poles might land south of the river facing the town. By then, I trusted, Arnhem would be in our hands and the flak batteries for which the RAF showed so much respect would be silenced. I also selected supply dropping zones.

I decided to put the 1st Parachute Brigade and the bulk of the 1st Airlanding Brigade down with the first lift, which would also include my own HQ and some divisional troops. Before the main force, the Independent Company would drop in order to mark the arrival areas. The Company had twelve Pathfinder aircraft, and there were 143 Dakotas from the 9th US Troop Carrier Command for the parachutists of the 1st Parachute Brigade, and 358 tugs and their equivalent in gliders for the rest. In the second lift, which would arrive twenty-four hours later, the main body of the 4th Parachute Brigade would jump from 126 Dakotas while the remainder of the Airlanding Brigade and other divisional units would land in 301 gliders. On the third day, I intended to bring in the main body of the 1st Polish Parachute Brigade in 114 Dakotas and thirty-five gliders.

At five o'clock on Tuesday afternoon, September 12th, I called a conference to give out my plan to my O Group, which included the brigade commanders, the brigade majors, the commanders of the gunners and sappers, and the heads of services – RASC, doctors, REME, RAOC. After the briefing had started, Freddie Gough, a cheerful, red-faced, silver-haired major who commanded the Reconnaissance Squadron, turned up with the air of a truant playing schoolboy and I laid into him afterwards for his unpunctuality. It was not the first time he had been very late for a conference. I thought nothing more of the incident, but I was to be reminded of it at the height of the battle.

Briefly, I explained to the assembled officers that I wanted the 1st Parachute Brigade to capture and hold the main road bridge in Arnhem and the pontoon bridge farther west. The 1st Airlanding Brigade would protect the dropping and landing zones until the second lift was on the ground and would then move east to form the left sector of the bridge-head on the western outskirts of Arnhem. The 4th Parachute Brigade would move eastwards on arrival and form the northern part of the position along the high ground north of the town, linking up with the 1st Parachute Brigade on the

22

Arnhem–Appeldoorn road. The 1st Polish Parachute Brigade under Sosabowski would land immediately south of the town, cross by the main bridge, which we should have captured by that time, and occupy the eastern outskirts of Arnhem.

I visualized a box-shaped bridgehead with standing patrols in advance of the main positions covering the bridge area.

Confirmatory notes on the orders were now given out and I went through them again, answering questions. There were very few. Generally, the brigadiers appeared not unhappy with the task confronting us and they now dispersed to make their own brigade plans.

I felt that I could hardly have been more fortunate in my brigadiers, and this was to be amply borne out in the battle. All three brigade commanders and the chief gunner, who later became a brigadier, were strikingly different. Gerald Lathbury, commanding the 1st Parachute Brigade, was tall and lithe with a languid method of speaking which tended to hide his extremely intelligent mind and clear brain. He had passed through the Staff College just before the war and in 1941, early in the development of airborne forces, had been posted to command the 3rd Parachute Battalion. He had taken over command of the 1st Parachute Brigade in 1943, leading it in Sicily where he was dropped wide of the rear of the brigade and was wounded after reaching the objective. Now, he had the 1st, 2nd and 3rd Battalions in his Brigade.

Pip Hicks, commanding the 1st Airlanding Brigade, was a solid infantryman who had belonged to the Royal Warwickshire Regiment. He had commanded the Airlanding Brigade in North Africa and in Sicily where his glider came down in the sea some miles off shore. Hicks had to swim for it, but eventually managed to take part in the battle. I think this experience had shaken him more than he suspected, but he was still an excellent commander much liked by his men. He used to get his leg pulled by his staff for his fondness for going on leave. Yet he was fundamentally a stolid and solemn individual with a reserved personality befitting the oldest man in the division: he was to spend his forty-ninth birthday at Arnhem. His brigade consisted of battalions of the Border Regiment, South Staffords and KOSB.

The commander of the 4th Parachute Brigade, Shan Hackett, was a remarkable little man with a pugilist's nose, sharp alert eyes and a personality which can only be called vivid. He had served with special forces in the desert and took over the 4th Parachute Brigade when it was formed. It was not an easy command. The 10th Battalion had been formed on a regular battalion of the Royal Sussex Regiment; the 11th Battalion consisted of drafts from various units in the Middle East, and the 156th Battalion was raised in India. Hackett had started life in the 8th Hussars and had not as much experience as the other two brigade commanders in infantry training. He was, however, a wonderful leader and as gallant as any man I have ever met. He had read a lot and was to make a habit of collecting degrees from the local university in whatever country he happened to be serving.

Our chief gunner, Robert Loder-Symonds, had already done well in the desert with the Horse Gunners, collecting two DSOs, though he had been badly wounded in the process. Even now he walked with a pronounced limp which, however, did not prevent him from getting around. There were times when he must have felt his wound most painfully. Robert was only thirty-one. He had an extremely high personal standard of behaviour, workmanship and morale. I was to see a lot of him during the perimeter fighting, as he was the most senior officer at my headquarters and we had many discussions about the situation in general. It was tragic and a terrible waste that Robert was later killed when taking off on an aerial reconnaissance in Java after the surrender of the Japanese.

Gerald Lathbury knew how vital it was to get a good start and everything in the beginning depended on his brigade. He decided that the Recce Squadron under Freddie Gough should try to take the main bridge by a *coup de main* and should come through the town to its target from the north-west. The 2nd Battalion was to push through Heelsum south of the dropping zone along the road hard by the river bank – 'the lower road' as it became known. At the bridge the battalion would take up defensive positions on both banks. The 3rd Battalion was to take the higher road from Heelsum into Arnhem, move on the bridge from the north, and then strengthen the bridge defence on the north-east. The 1st Battalion was not to make for the bridge at all, but for the high ground north of the town – and then only when it was clear that the other two battalions were advancing towards the bridge. By the end of the first day, it was hoped that the 1st Battalion would hold an outer line with a strong inner defensive ring consisting of the 2nd and 3rd Battalions.

This fitted neatly into the divisional plan.

There were late modifications caused mainly by changes in the number of aircraft available to us. And on Thursday, September 14th, I went off in my own Oxford aircraft to look round the division, which was scattered over the southern half of England. As I looked down on the camps and airfields now being prepared for 'Market Garden' I was reminded of my own quite brief association with the division. One evening late in December 1943 General Sir Neil Ritchie, my corps commander, had summoned me to his caravan and told me of a message he had received from the Commander-in-Chief Home Forces to the effect that I was shortly to be given command of the 1st Airborne Division. It came as a great surprise; I had no previous experience of airborne operations, and had given no thought to them, and I was also subject at times to airsickness. Some flights made me feel very ill, and the worst of these was on a flight from Durban to Cairo on the way up to the desert when I was on the staff of the 51st Highland Division. Having been lavishly entertained by well-meaning acquaintances in Durban, I was already feeling slightly less than robust when we took off very early in the morning. Conditions were bumpy, and I was feeling very low and conscious of my own pallor when my divisional commander, General Wimberley, tapped me on the shoulder and remarked: 'You're not looking too well. Look out of the window. It's a lovely sight below.' I glanced down at a green-fringed lake, and instantly had to make an exit.

However, the physical handicap was a minor one compared with the attraction of my first divisional command. I had commanded 231 Independent Brigade Group in Sicily and Italy and had served with the Highland Division in the Desert.

I had only been in my present appointment as Brigadier General Staff, at XII Corps for a few months after being slightly wounded in Italy. Whenever I did wonder about the prospects of my commanding a division, the last thing that entered my head was that it would be airborne. I had no ideas at all how these chaps functioned, and my impression was that airborne forces had been run rather as a family business and as a private army, and had up to date generally produced their own senior officers.

What was unknown to me at this stage was that Major-General Eric Down, a soldier saturated in airborne experience following his successive commands of the 1st Parachute Battalion, the 2nd Parachute Brigade, and then the 1st Airborne Division, was needed in the Far East to raise an Indian airborne division. I learned long afterwards that Boy Browning had contested this posting only to be overruled by the War Office. Browning had then been asked, 'Do you mind having a chap from outside for the 1st Airborne Division?'

'He must be hot from the battle,' Browning insisted.

It was thus that I called on Browning in the New Year of 1944 at his HQ near St James's Court. I was still wearing a brigadier's badges and the tartan trews and spats of the HLI. Browning, who has the appearance of a restless hawk with his sharp nose and small alert eyes, greeted me briskly and observed: 'You had better go and get yourself properly dressed.'

I was very much aware of my lack of experience of airborne operations, of my air travel weakness, and also of the fact that I'd never even parachuted or travelled by glider in my life. Nevertheless, it seemed to me that the basic rules were the same. An airborne division was a force of highly-trained infantry, with the usual gunner and sapper support, and once it had descended from the sky it resorted to normal ground fighting. Infantry rules operated, if under rather different conditions, especially in the early stages of a battle when the force was almost certain to be on its own.

I suggested to Browning that I might take some parachute training. He surveyed my bulk – I was six feet and more than fourteen stone at the time – and said: 'I shouldn't worry about learning to parachute. Your job is to prepare this division for the invasion of Europe. Not only are you too big for parachuting but you are also getting on.' I was forty-two. He leaned back in his chair, a lithe and dapper man, and drumming his fingers on the desk said: 'I did two jumps. Hurt myself both times. I was terrified of breaking something.' He smiled, it seemed, at the memory of some half-forgotten incident. 'I was the only one who knew anything about this business – so I became a glider pilot.'

Thus reassured I went off to meet my predecessor, Eric Down, at the Naval and Military Club for lunch. He was unhappy about the new arrangement but wished me well and told me about the division's 'background' and its personalities.

On January 7th, 1944, I drove to Fulbeck to take over the division. I was received with some surprise and a good deal of curiosity, and I was soon to learn that an airborne division is a rather self-contained community into which one has to be accepted. I was clearly a military landlubber. I was aware of being looked over closely with ill-concealed reservations in some quarters. I had plenty to overcome. To make the situation rather more complicated, one of the brigadiers had been given to understand unofficially that he would be given command.

As winter gave way to spring, the divisional preparations reached an advanced state. Just before an exercise with the 6th Airborne Division I had an infuriating attack of malaria. It laid me low for three weeks and by the time I recovered D-Day in Normandy was approaching.

Only one British airborne division was required in the initial assault – and the 6th, under Richard Gale, was chosen to drop on the left flank of the Normandy bridgehead. We were labelled 'strategic reserve' and were expected to move at short notice. Then developed what can only be called our own 'phoney war' in which we were due to go into action on sixteen different occasions only to have the operations rendered unnecessary either by the swift advance of the ground armies across the Continent or by their inability to make enough progress. Some were cancelled because of second thoughts as to the feasibility of the plans. First, it was planned to drop

Shan Hackett and the 4th Parachute Brigade on the D-Day beaches. Next, I prepared for the entire division to do a similar beach landing in case of emergency.

Throughout that hot, exciting summer, operational plans tumbled one over the other. In the main we were left frustrated and disappointed; but there were times when I felt relief at certain cancellations. Such an occasion was the plan to send us in ahead of the beachhead at Evrecy. It would have been a sticky battle, and Operation 'Wild Oats' was aptly named. There was the time when, in conjunction with the Navy, we were to take St Malo; but the Navy discovered seaside deterrents to their role, and it was considered too well-defended a stronghold to be cracked entirely from the land alone.

In 'Raising Britanny' we were to form a base in Britanny for the Maquis with whom we were to join in operations against the flank of the German Army preliminary to a link up with the Americans moving south from the Cherbourg Peninsula. In 'Hands Up' we were to take Vannes north of the mouth of the Loire; in 'Sword Hilt' the Morlaix-Lannon area of north Britanny; in 'Transfigure' we were to rendezvous with the Americans who were engaged in a right hook to take Paris. Twice there were plans for our establishing bridgeheads across the Seine, below Rouen and then at Les Andelys, and we were twice to be hurled ahead of the advancing armies in Belgium.

Then came 'Comet'. In this operation, we were to seize the three river crossings in the Netherlands along the projected axis of 2nd Army – the Maas, the Waal and the Neder Rhine. It was certainly taking a chance because of the wide dispersal involved and also because of our ignorance of German movements on the ground in the area. We were all becoming increasingly aware of a certain naïveté in upper level planning of airborne operations, particularly at the HQ of the 1st Allied Airborne Army. I recall one conference during the preparations for 'Comet', when both Shan Hackett and General Sosabowski, commanding the Polish Brigade which was under my command for the operation, reacted strongly. Sosabowski, who had been a professor at Warsaw War

Academy, interrupted several times as I explained the plan which had come down to us. 'But the Germans, General . . . the Germans!' More and more we saw that German reactions had not been taken into account at all.

Sosabowski visualized them clearly enough, and so determined was he to come to grips on a footing at least equal to that held by an enemy which had overrun and ravaged his own country, that his protestations were not born of despair so much as of rage that a victory might be denied us because of a lack of foresight in planning.

A very highly trained soldier, Sosabowski was also a character with a vengeance. Like most of the Poles, he had a natural courtesy which contrasted violently with the sudden outbursts in speech and temper which positively withered any erring individual of whose behaviour or methods he did not approve. Nevertheless, when during the months of training I visited his brigade several times, I soon found that he not only had the affection of his men, but was tremendously respected by all those who served with him – two attitudes to a commander which in my experience have not always gone hand-in-hand together.

He was, of course, a political leader as well, a role which led him into queer paths. There were times when I could not be certain whether he was debating a point from the military angle or merely trying to put over the Polish political cause. He fell out badly with General Browning on two or three occasions, and even at the end their relations were not of the best.

None of the operations planned before 'Market Garden' came to anything: two of them might have been utterly disastrous. They had the effect, however, of sharpening our state of readiness and advancing our planning to a fine art, and also of creating a common attitude of eagerness to be off. By September 1944 my division was battle-hungry to a degree which only those who have commanded large forces of trained soldiers can fully comprehend. In fact, there were already signs of that dangerous mixture of boredom and cynicism creeping into our daily lives. We were ready for anything. If there was a tendency to take light-heartedly the less encouraging factors, and even the unknown ones, it was understandable. Certainly, it is impossible to over-emphasize the ultimate significance of this process of operations that never were. In the cold afterlight the historian and military critic has his licence to juggle the arithmetical equations of battle. Only the participant can adequately apportion the invisible factors, such as the effects of the sixteen cancelled operations in a row.

It was Friday, September 15th. While the troops were being briefed at the airfields and others had begun to load the gliders, I took out my golf clubs and played a few of those holes still usable at Moor Park. At one of them I was just about to putt when I saw Mackenzie standing on the edge of the green. He was concerned about something but seemed prepared to wait until I had holed my putt. 'What is it, Charles?' I said. 'Go on talking.'

Mackenzie said there had been a reduction of a few gliders and we would have to cut our load on the first lift. I told him: 'Whatever is to be sacrificed it must not be anti-tank guns.' Despite the optimistic reports from the British Army across the Channel I was not taking more chances than were necessary as regards the German armour. We would need every anti-tank weapon we could lay hands on.

Mackenzie acknowledged the point.

I holed out.

Unknown to us, the Germans were reorganizing – both ahead of the 2nd Army and at Arnhem. In Holland, the Army Group B commander, Field-Marshal Model, a German senior officer of the old school, squat, broad-beamed and wearing a monocle, issued an order on September 9th to the 10th SS Panzer Division (known as the Frundsberg) to keep going in its rearward move past Arnhem into Germany. He also ordered General Willi Bittrich to prepare the 9th SS Panzer Division (Hohenstaufen) for a move against the Americans near Aachen. Bittrich, a straight-backed career officer who commanded the II SS Panzer Corps, had earlier been ordered by Model to direct the rehabilitation of the 9th and two other panzer divisions, the 2nd and the 116th.

To understand fully the German position in Holland at this stage it is necessary to go back to Normandy. In that flaming June Bittrich had under command the 9th and 10th SS Panzer Divisions. Among German soldiers they were regarded as crack formations and one senior German officer was to tell me that he thought they were inferior only to the Alpine and Hermann Goering Divisions. By June 10th both divisions were engaged in costly counter-attacks against the beachhead and were stopped by what has since been described as 'a terrible curtain of artillery'. On that day, it became clear to many German officers of these divisions that the Allies were bound to win. Despite the propaganda about the success of the flying bombs and promises of other super weapons, even the sternly Nazi officers of the Waffen SS knew that Germany was on the verge of the abyss. As his troops were blasted by artillery and rocket-firing Typhoons, Bittrich himself realized this. He and his troops summoned up a 'courage of despair'.

When Bittrich ordered his corps to counter-attack an important area of high ground south-west of Caen, and nothing happened, he appeared in a Volkswagen, standing upright, statuesque and apparently unmoved by the shelling that had forced his troops to take cover. He shouted orders which made them get up and advance. A tall, handsome German officer in the classical mould, Bittrich had a reputation among his subordinates for gentle manners and a sense of humour. Once he had studied to be a conductor. During the First World War he had served in a regiment which had later thrown up many senior officers and henchmen of Hitler. At one point between the wars he had been transferred to the Luftwaffe and served in a unit with Goering, whom he is said to have despised. He had for a time helped in the training of the Luftwaffe in great secrecy in Russia. He liked to talk about Rommel, of whom he was a firm admirer. There is conflicting evidence of Bittrich's political background and how he came to be a Waffen SS general, which is irrelevant in this account. What matters is that Bittrich had tremendous professional ability as a soldier which he was to exploit to the full during the battle of Arnhem.

During lulls in the battle in Normandy and later, he used to summon three of his staff officers for a game of bridge. Sometimes they played in his staff car and occasionally in a French chateau by candlelight with a bottle of champagne on the table. On one of these occasions when the Allied superiority was being felt, Bittrich remarked: 'If the British are going to capture us, they should at least capture us playing bridge.'

In Normandy the 2nd Army had come close to knocking Bittrich's command from under him. The SS troops had a rough time at the hands of the Guards Armoured Division while from the air Typhoons of the 2nd Tactical Air Force were catching the convoys under the slight screen of trees at the river crossings and on the roads out of Normandy. The retreat cost Bittrich and his men most of their heavy equipment as well as loot and their own personal belongings. When the commander of the Hohenstaufen Division was wounded his command was taken over by Oberführer Colonel Bloch, an artillery commander who had no guns left to command.

Never had a master race theory appeared more stupid than it did now to these Germans. Physically exhausted and short of sleep and food they were for a change in the role of the hunted. They were now harried so that they had not time even to change their clothing. 'For weeks', a German officer on Bittrich's staff later told me, 'we slept with our boots on – and it was too much even for the battle-hardened troops in our command.' Their communications were wrecked and they were withdrawing in disorder towards the Reich. Even the Germans saw in this chaotic flight evidence of the last road out. During the retreat Monty summoned Browning to the Continent, and Browning flew over in a Mosquito. Given the whereabouts of Monty's HQ he borrowed a jeep. At that time the Guards Armoured Division was thrusting towards Brussels and on the road Browning came up against the rear of a convoy of lorries. He sounded his horn impatiently and from the rear lorry a helmet emerged. 'I had a considerable surprise,' said Browning. 'It was a German helmet.' He slipped down the next turning.

As the 9th and 10th SS Panzer Divisions withdrew through Holland they heard on the radio from Germany that Heinrich

PARATROOPS BOARDING A DAKOTA

PARATROOPS JUMPING

PART OF A GLIDER LANDING ZONE

THE MAIN DROPPING ZONE

A 6-POUNDER ANTI-TANK GUN IN ACTION

A 3-INCH MORTAR TEAM

THE REMAINS OF A GERMAN ARMOURED COLUMN WHICH TRIED TO RUSH THE BRIDGE FROM THE SOUTH

Himmler had been appointed General-in-Chief of the Western Front and that he was building a defence line along the German border.

Momentarily the tempo of the retreat eased.

If such a high-ranking Nazi was prepared to take on the job surely it could not be hopeless? Thus ran the thoughts of the German troops, though the reality was that only armoured divisions counted now, and all were heavily engaged either in battle or retreat.

On the wide main road approaching Nijmegen Bridge beyond Grave the disorganized and retreating Germans were met and sorted out by relays of officers and military police. The SS men, with their stripes and divisional names on their sleeves, were easily assembled. The 9th SS Panzer Division was concentrated north of Arnhem and the 10th in the neighbourhood of Nijmegen. And on September 3rd Field-Marshal Model issued the order that was to alter markedly our prospects. On that day he directed that the 9th and 10th Divisions were to move to the Arnhem area for rehabilitation. By September 5th he had modified this order to give Bittrich control of the rehabilitation of the 9th, with the 2nd and 116th Divisions, then engaged further south, also under his command. Model had other things in mind for the 10th Division. It was to keep going into Germany for the refit, while the 9th prepared to move against the Americans.

As our D-Day drew near, these SS divisions were still in the Arnhem area.

Immediately ahead of the 2nd Army, the Germans were similarly pulling themselves together. It was estimated that XXX Corps might reach the Zuider Zee, ninety-nine miles from the start line, between two and five days after crossing the Dutch-Belgian border. They were expected to link up with us in Arnhem between the second and fourth days – a distance of sixty-four miles. It seemed hardly over-optimistic considering that between the end of August and September 11th the 2nd Army had advanced some 280 miles from the River Seine to the Escaut Canal. Yet it needed no military genius to detect the snags. Firstly, the advance was planned along a very narrow front with only one highway most of the distance, through Eindhoven, St Oedenrode, Veghel, Uden, Grave, Nijmegen, Arnhem and Apeldoorn. It was difficult tank country and yet the operation depended largely on the mobility of the Guards Armoured Division, which had the support of the 43rd and 50th Infantry Divisions of General Horrocks's XXX Corps. On Horrocks's right would be VIII Corps and on his left XII Corps. Already the lines of communication were strained: the very speed of events since June had meant that no intermediate ports were functioning between the front line and Caen. The railways were mostly unserviceable – and the logistical situation as a whole was far from healthy.

The Germans were trying desperately to bolt the door. After the fall of Antwerp, Hitler had personally ordered General Student and the HQ of the 1st Parachute Army to the Dutch-Belgian frontier. Student had under his command the 88th Corps under General Reinhard and the 719th Infantry Division under Generalleutnant Sievers. Reinhard, gambling on the main British attack taking place on the western stretch of the Albert Canal, concentrated his Corps there. He calculated that the British might attempt a drive north to seal off Walcheren and the Zuid Baevelend Peninsula, thereby trapping finally the German 15th Army which might otherwise escape across the Scheldt Estuary. In addition, the British would thereby clear the seaward approaches to Antwerp without which the port was useless. Monty's plan, however, was much more ambitious than Reinhard reckoned and it would have meant that the 2nd Army drive would hit the German line at its weakest point but for a somewhat fortuitous intervention. The German 85th Division, battered and in retreat, was halted by its commander, Generalleutnant Chill, in mid-withdrawal and placed defensively along the canal. Chill, who had seen the dangerous situation developing there for the Germans, rounded up other soldiers from every section of the Wehrmacht as well as sailors and Luftwaffe men caught up in the receding tide. It was this force, so desperately gathered, which held off the first XXX Corps probes in the canal area. And when XXX Corps got their feet over the canal at Beeringen, Chill was given the task of stopping them.

Student now had a makeshift line of troops which had come almost from nowhere and in the next twenty-four hours the 176th Division filled in the line. Presently Student's own paratroops took their places.

Thus by mid-September, as the 2nd Army paused in readiness for 'Market Garden', it was firmly faced by the Germans' 1st Parachute Army. In addition the German 15th Army had been slipping out of the coastal trap to be ferried across the estuary of the Scheldt. From his HQ in a white-fronted hotel in open grounds at Oosterbeek near Arnhem, Model controlled both these armies and also exercised command over the local defence forces in the Netherlands. A Luftwaffe General, Christiansen, was responsible for relations with the Wehrmacht and for the protection of military installations, rail centres and supply dumps. Under the new set-up he was charged with the defence of all territory north of the River Maas. He had under his command a conglomeration of regional defence and support men from the Waffen SS, the Wehrmacht, the Navy and the Luftwaffe.

There was another force which the Germans could muster; the last-ditch troops of Wehrkreis VI, the territorial command which embraced that province of Germany closest to our chosen battle area. They were popularly known among the German troops as the 'ear and stomach battalions' because of their medical categories.

If besides the 1st Parachute Army there had been only those divisions escaping from across the Scheldt, the Armed Forces Command Netherlands and Wehrkreis VI, 'Market Garden' would probably have worked perfectly. Unfortunately for us, between Nijmegen and Arnhem, and in Arnhem itself, and under cover of the woods north-east of Arnhem, there were the tanks and self-propelled guns of the 9th and 10th SS Panzer Divisions.

As the critical weekend approached, few of them had started to roll into Germany.

With our preparations complete and the staff dispersed from Moor Park to the Airfields, I tried to picture the situation around the dropping and landing zone. The lack of intelligence was a nuisance, but hardly more than that. We had waited patiently for this opportunity and most of us were hoping that there would be no call on the scrambler telephone from Browning with a cancellation. As the weekend came on, I began to think that this time the operation would come off. Between tying up points in the plan with the various brigades and studying maps and the latest reconnaissance photos, and trying to get more information out of Corps, I had a few holes of golf with my ADC, Graham Roberts. A tidy, round-faced youngster with a serious disposition, Roberts shared a pent-house outside my caravan on the Moor Park course with my RAF pilot. We were parked under a large elm facing a fair-way, and several times we had played against General Paul Williams, commander of the 9th US Troop Carrier Com-mand, and his ADC. They had challenged us to a rubber of three matches. We won the first and they took the second. Roberts now reminded me that it looked as if the thing would remain a draw.

On the Friday night the staff officers remaining decided to have a party to celebrate the occasion. I was invited but chose not to go. Senior officers sometimes have an unnecessarily restricting influence on such occasions. Returning from the party, Major Tiny Madden, who was on my staff, was involved in a bad smash and was taken to hospital. It didn't keep him away from Arnhem.

Saturday, September 16th, dawned crisp and clear. The bustle had gone from Moor Park. In the late afternoon we were due to fly to the airfield from which the divisional HQ would take off with the first lift next day. My own Oxford was at Cranwell, and the pilot had orders to fly it to Brussels as soon as the operation began. Graham Roberts laid on another air-craft for our journey to Fairford. A hitch developed, and we were kept waiting at a small airfield adjoining Denham golf course. Roberts came over to me, somewhat concerned, and said: 'I'm sorry, sir, but everything is not going quite accord-ing to plan.'

'If this is the worst thing that's going to happen,' I replied, 'we'll be all right.'

Another snag actually had arisen since we had left Moor

Park. We had asked for a preliminary air attack on a lunatic asylum which I could see from the map was uncomfortably close to our assembly points just south of Wolfhezen station. As he was about to leave Moor Park, Mackenzie was called to the telephone. It was a senior officer of the US Air Force, who wanted a personal assurance from me that there were Germans in the asylum and not lunatics. The Americans who were to bomb the place would not do so unless we took responsibility.

Mackenzie thought for a moment of the consequences of his decision and recalled our brief conversation about the asylum and its probable present occupants.

'We consider there are Germans in it,' Mackenzie said.

'And you will take responsibility?'

'I take responsibility,' he said.

'On your head be it,' came the reply.

The attack was fixed for an hour before we began to arrive.

As we flew down to the West Country to our airfield, Roberts, my batman Hancock and I looked down in the fading light of early evening on the airfields from which the men of the division would be going into battle tomorrow. The tugs and gliders, with their freshly painted white stripes across the wings and fuselage, resembled swarms of patient bees. Close by, the troops waited, keyed up, in the tented camps.

I joined in a game of bridge, and heard a poker session in progress in a nearby tent.

I went to bed early.

As dawn came up on our D-Day I was already wide awake. The padre conducted a communion service on the airfield, and I had breakfast alone in the mess. On the airfield, the men were clustering round their aircraft – a positive jam of aircraft. Walking among the men I recalled General Horrocks's somewhat strange words to me when we had been discussing my division during the planning of a previous operation in France. 'Your men are killers,' Horrocks had said. A slight overstatement, but in their battlesmocks and crash helmets they looked now like a force that would be capable of big

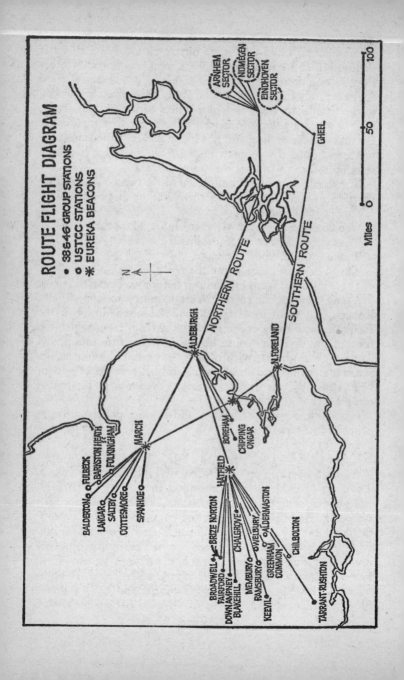

things against the enemy. Every team was thoroughly shaken down. The men of the glider units now stood alongside their Horsas and the more bulky and vulnerable looking Hamilcars with their loads of heavy gear ranging from 17-pounder anti-tank guns to Bren carriers. In our glider there were Graham Roberts, Hancock, a signaller, two military policemen whose function was to escort me, my jeep, and the MPs' motor-cycles. We had done several test landings without mishap.

I wished Boy Wilson good luck. This tough, incorrigibly eager little men who, at forty-five, was the oldest parachutist in the division, was positively boyish now that he was about to set off in the van of the armada.

His appetite for a fight had enlivened many a discussion in the months of waiting. Wilson was rather possessive about his hand-picked company, the pathfinder force. He had always been rather proud of the fact that his men had captured the Italian port of Bari. When I joined the division I was advised that Wilson was a provocative individualist who knew as much about parachute soldiering as anyone still alive. His association with airborne operations dated to the time when Browning had taken over the making of the 1st Airborne Division. Browning decided that gliders would not be able to land without the aid of men on the ground who could put out smoke and lay coloured panels as signals for the pilots, and mark out a landing path.

It was a specially select unit which was also equipped with Eureka radar.

Wilson had been wounded as a reservist in France and was with a Home Defence unit in Wales when he heard of Browning's new job and wrote asking to be allowed to join the new airborne force.

Browning agreed on condition that Wilson was medically fit. It was common knowledge in the division that Wilson had had a defective ear and that when the medical officer checked his healthy one, Wilson had drawn his attention to some small incident outside and had then offered the same ear for examination. Wilson and company not only led the force but conducted a good deal of experimental work including the testing of new parachutes and modifications involving new paratroop carrying aircraft or jump techniques.

I recalled my first meeting with Wilson soon after I took command. Modestly built, he oozed a confidence and assertiveness out of proportion to his size which compelled me to remark: 'Ah Wilson. I understand you bounce off everybody.'

'Sir,' he replied formally and without diffidence, 'I have an independent unit and I'm considered to be rather independent.'

Later I was to hear much from Wilson and others about his remarkable collection of highly intelligent, battle-crusted men. Among them were twenty-five Jewish ex-refugees recruited partly for their command of the German language but also for their magnificent fighting qualities. In advance of the operation, they had all taken new names to avoid identification should they fall into German hands – and the names were Scottish and most of them began with Mac.

Wilson and the 186 officers and men with him were due to spend half an hour in the area on their own before the rest of the division started to come in. They had to mark four dropping zones and five glider landing areas, using Eureka radar and smoke signals.

It was a glorious lazy Sunday, fine and clear except for some broken cumulus cloud. The refreshment vans were busy among the aircraft. Many of the troops were taking copies of that morning's Sunday papers. Some were chalking symbols and rude remarks on their gliders. At airfields all over the southern half of England the scene was the same; revving engines, orderly streams of bombers and gliders, groups of men enjoying their last cup of tea in England, cracking jokes, and wondering deep down what faced us on the other side.

As a precaution, I mentioned to Charles Mackenzie that if I were put out of the battle Lathbury should take command of the division with Hicks and Hackett succeeding in that order. I had a few final words with Robert Loder-Symonds, who was limping around with wonderful zest.

I climbed aboard the Horsa in which already the rest of the passengers had taken their places. In front sat Colonal Iain

Murray, commander of one of the two glider wings involved, and his co-pilot. I had a small shoulder pack containing my shaving gear and other odds and ends including chocolate. Hancock, a little Cornishman who had been with me since early in 1941, through the desert, Sicily and Italy, and who now wore a red beret with great pride, had made a practice of giving me his chocolate out of the ration in exchange for my cigarettes, as I was a non-smoker. In my jeep I had another pack with a clean shirt, a change of underclothes, and a bottle of whisky. I carried a map case, one map of the Arnhem area, a notebook, and inside my smock, two grenades. Even so, I seemed to be heavily laden and I felt sympathy for those parachutists who were to be seen hobbling with gear which included leaden-looking leg-bags containing heavier weapons – Brens, mortar parts and Vickers machine-guns. Others, looking even more weighed down, had valises across their chests containing weapons and ammunition.

I rummaged finally through my pockets to check that I was carrying no information which could be of use to the enemy; we were security conscious to a man and there was not a soldier who didn't realize that to forget or to disobey the order not to take operational instructions into the air could cost his own and others' lives.

I strapped myself in, exchanged a word with Hancock, and glanced around the inside of the glider. I felt the slight jolt as the tow-rope took the strain. Hancock was regarding me with some slight concern: he knew, as did so many members of the division, all about my capacity for airsickness.

As we took off, an orderly was laying out the table for lunch in the ground floor dining-room of the Hartenstein Hotel at Oosterbeek, used by the staff of Model's tactical HQ at Oosterbeek. Model himself was already immersed in planning the reorganized German defence of Holland. In Arnhem, city dwellers living near the great parabola of steel over the Neder Rhine which was our chief target were taking a mid-morning stroll. Others were on their way to church. Mrs Kate Ter Horst and her family were leaving their rectangular white house hard by the polder skirting the river for the Oosterbeek village church next door. On the high ground north-west of Arnhem a farmer was standing by the door of his farmhouse taking in the clean warm air and gazing out across his deserted potato fields.

Fifty Mosquitos, forty-eight Mitchells and twenty-four Bostons were flying in for attacks on barracks at Arnhem, Nijmegen and Ede. Among the assigned targets was the lunatic asylum at Wolfhezen. An SS major set out on a bicycle looted from France for a ride round the open country north-west of Arnhem. Other German troops, taking advantage of the breathing space they had been given, were out walking.

It was a still, lazy day – and the sun was shining.

# CHAPTER TWO

OUR ARRIVAL was deceptively peaceful. As Iain Murray started his landing glide, I gazed over his shoulder at the ordered, brown and green landscape below, where already many gliders now lay. Others, as they touched down, kicked up clouds of dust from the dry, sandy earth. I could see the troops hastily assembling their jeeps and guns and making for cover; here and there was a Dutch family on the way home from church.

Not a shot was being fired.

I liked the look of this landing zone – flat, spacious, and sheltered by the screens of pine woods. A few gliders had somersaulted, and I noticed that one Horsa had careered into the pines fringing the patchwork of potato and turnip fields and heather moor.

The flight had been relatively uneventful. We took off at the rate of one a minute from Fairford, and flew around while the air columns formed up in their prearranged battle order. For almost two hours we were over England and Wales, first going northwards over the Severn and then across the Midlands towards the North Sea. Our last sight of England was the Norfolk coast, clearly outlined below now that the slight morning mist had dispersed. The sun was coming out. I glanced ahead and below where I could see four other tugs and their gliders and, on an uncommonly calm sea, the air-sea rescue craft stationed for our greater safety at comforting intervals. Anyone who fell into the sea would have a good chance of survival. Presently when the towrope snapped between one tug and its glider I saw air-sea rescue vessels moving smartly towards the ditched glider. Another Horsa went down, a Mitchell bomber in some trouble passed us going the other way, and then we were over the coast of Holland.

I had expected flak hereabouts, but none came.

American and RAF fighters had been assigned a tremendous task in the preceding twenty-four hours in accordance with

43

the promises made by Browning who had finally prevailed on the RAF to co-operate in a daylight assault. Holland was thick with flak batteries. Long-range American fighters escorting Flying Fortresses were dousing them all the way along the air routes, and we went into Holland with a combined RAF and American fighter escort of 1200 aircraft. Only twice were Luftwaffe fighters encountered – fifteen Me 109s north of Wesel and a similar number of Focke Wulf 190s south-west of the same town. They were well out of harm's reach. For much of the way, I stood behind Murray and his co-pilot following the flight plan. Near Hertogenbosch we turned north-east for Arnhem, leaving the 82nd and 101st Divisions on a different track for their roles at Grave and Nijmegen.

As we flew in, it was interesting to find the area conforming to the pictures I had built up in my mind, based on the maps and aerial photographs. First I had picked out the line of the Neder Rhine, then the rail and road bridges, and now the pine woods, the level crossing and the tall chimney-stack of Wolfhezen. Two columns of smoke issued from the lunatic asylum at Wolfhezen and the barracks at Ede; testimony to the aerial strikes that had preceded our arrival.

Yet the landing zone was untroubled. As we descended, a Horsa ahead to our left landed awkwardly, stirring dust, and pitched over on its nose. A Hamilcar somersaulted; another slewed as it touched down, straightened, appeared to be going over and then righted itself. I saw one glider finish up among the trees, its wings snapped like twigs. We were about half a mile from the landing zone when the tug shook us off; I was fascinated watching the rope falling away from the nose of the glider and still attached to the tug aircraft.

Now we could see the smoke signals and yellow markers laid out by Boy Wilson's men, whose earlier appearance had provoked hardly any opposition. It was just like an exercise in Hampshire. So confident was the Independent Company about the outcome that they had taken quantities of metal and boot polish for the liberation celebrations and the victorious entry into Germany. Wilson had packed his best battledress and highly-polished brown shoes into his parachu-

44

tist's leg-bag which also contained one bottle each of whisky, gin and sherry for the entertainment of Dutch Resistance leaders. The leg-bag weighted seventy-five pounds, and the liquor was intact when Boy landed.

The Independent Company had begun jumping from the twelve Pathfinder Stirlings precisely at midday after an undisturbed flight. Glancing down through the aperture, Wilson saw cows grazing peacefully in the warm sunshine. Then the red light flickered, and they were away, falling through sparse small-arms fire. Of two men who were hit as they came down, one died and the other was unhurt although a bullet passed through his chest haversack which held mortar bombs. Wilson struggled clear of his harness to find himself face to face with a surrendering German, who led him to a foxhole occupied by other members of the Wehrmacht who saw little point in fighting. They had been having lunch when the attack had begun.

Wilson ordered the Germans to hang on while he organized his task force. He contacted his platoons by wireless and ordered the release of pigeons carrying messages to London with news of the unopposed landing. The birds settled on the farmhouse roof, however, and pebbles had to be thrown before they would take wing.

A quarter of an hour before the first gliders of the main force were due, Wilson's men were in position with one casualty, sixteen prisoners and their first booty – a German staff car. Nevertheless, Wilson felt uneasy and 'rather lonely' until the throb of the main force was heard. As the air columns came into view, he left the farm he was using as his HQ and prepared to help with the landings. One glider pilot took evasive action to avoid overshooting, and a wing hit the ground. The aircraft slewed, skidded, churned the pale earth, and tore apart. Wilson ran forward to assist. Men stumbled out of the machine, shaken and bruised and some of them with superficial gashes, but there was not a single serious casualty. Wilson recognized the pilot, an ex-Guardsman, as an old friend. 'Come along to my HQ,' he said. 'I'll give you some water.' In the farmhouse, Wilson opened his whisky bottle and poured out a drink. The pilot turned his blackened, scratched face towards his host and remarked: 'My God, this Dutch water's good!'

As we came in to land, the skill of the glider pilots was clear to see. Their thin-walled flying boxcars had skidded in all directions; some had been tucked into tight corners of the landing zone, sections of which were jammed like a car park. Most had landed in the right direction only to be forced to turn because of the congestion. Many pilots, cast-off beyond the optimum height, had circled in order to land in the right place.

We landed gently. I jumped out and left Hancock and the rest to get on with the unloading of my jeep. As the unloading went on, I walked over to the edge of the landing zone to watch the rest of the force arriving. Already, civilians were appearing in their Sunday best. The farmer whose home was bang in the middle of the zone talked animatedly to a group of gliderborne soldiers and pointed towards Arnhem as others commandeered his car. Jeeps, guns, small parties of men were moving off now; here and there soldiers were having trouble in salvaging their gear from the broken-backed gliders and I saw one group man-handling an anti-tank gun out of the smashed side of one aircraft. On the ground were the orange and crimson strips of nylon laid out by Wilson's party and pinioned by stones and sods of earth. From the depths of the wood behind, we heard a few desultory shots and a lot of shouting. I watched a party of troops moving off towards the new arterial road linking The Hague and Arnhem.

As the unloading progressed, we had a grandstand view of the 1st Parachute Brigade's drop some 400 yards away. The Dakotas were right on target, and parachutists filled the sky. I could see that hardly any of them were drifting astray and that it was turning out to be a textbook drop. My immediate concern was to see that everyone was getting on with his allotted task as quickly as possible. I had deliberately to restrain myself from interfering, for the stage was not yet when I could do much to help. At such times, generals are spectators. I went over to the dropping zone and watched the parachutists picking themselves up, collecting the valises which hit the ground first, and unpacking the mortars and machine-guns.

46

Ammunition, rations and heavier gear descended in supply containers which were located and collected with an urgency that further convinced me that everything was going our way.

Now, however, came the first intimation of a snag that was to grow and bedevil us almost to the end.

My tactical HQ was operational now under the trees on the edge of the wood, but the signallers were finding it difficult to raise anyone. We were soon to learn that our radio sets were inadequate for the purpose, and that their effectiveness was to be further limited by the sandy, heavily-wooded terrain. Information was scarce. I had seen enough to satisfy myself that Lathbury's 1st Brigade was all right, but there was no news of Hick's Airlanding Brigade which had landed north of our position. I decided to go off and check personally with Hicks. Just as I was about to leave with my signaller in the jeep, a number of civilians appeared in the wood: they were all smiles and full of greetings, and some just stared. We assumed, rightly as it turned out, that they were patients who had escaped from the asylum following the bombing. They looked none the worst for their experience, and did not interfere.

Hicks was away visiting his battalions when I reached his HQ. The brigade had arrived in good order, but I was given some disturbing news about the Recce Squadron. This mixed force of glider troops and parachutists which was to effect the *coup de main* against the Bridge had not even started, for the simple reason that among the gliders which had failed to arrive were those containing most of the squadron's vehicles. This part of the plan – the race for the Bridge – had gone completely awry. It was important now that I should make an alternative plan with Freddie Gough, commander of the Reconnaissance Squadron, and that Lathbury should be told that his 2nd Battalion, under John Frost, was now going hell-bent for the Bridge alone. There was the added snag that one troop of Gough's men were designed to work with my HQ, and that I now needed Gough to drive ahead of me towards the town. Nobody knew his whereabouts. I left orders that he should contact me immediately, and returned to my own HQ. Not only was there no news of

Gough when I got back but the communications were a complete failure. Some short-range inter-unit exchanges were going on, but the 1st Parachute Brigade, and the outside world, had not been contacted.

Signals failures were no new phenomenon. I had known them often enough in the desert, and had learned the value of personal mobility at such times. It was now getting on in the afternoon, and the Germans were reacting. A few mortar bombs had been dropped in the area, and the HQ personnel were digging slit trenches. I calculated that Lathbury's brigade, even after the efficient start I had seen them make, could not yet have reached the Bridge. I had seen some jeeps setting off, but most of the men were footslogging and they could not have been going much more than a couple of hours. Leaving instructions for Gough to contact me at Lathbury's HQ, which was following the 2nd Battalion on the lower road, I now set off in the jeep with my signaller trying to raise Gough on the rover set in the back seat. He had one set of headphones, and another set lay on the seat beside me. I made for the southern road where John Frost and the 2nd Battalion were presumably heading for the Bridge. It was essential that I should get some idea of their progress and also make it clear that they could no longer rely on Gough and the Recce boys being at the Bridge. I drove down a cindered track to a secondary road and soon came upon the Arnhem–Utrecht highway, modern and tree-fringed with wide sandy avenues between the roadside conifers and the gardens of the prosperous villas. Along the road came a file of subdued Germans guarded by one paratrooper who saluted and grinned hugely as I passed. Across the main road, I turned right into a winding, narrow descent towards the river. There was no activity, though we could hear the sound of shooting coming from the direction of the town. What struck me now was the undulating nature of the country, which was not unfavourable to defence, and the height of the wire-mesh fences surrounding many of the houses; factors which were likely to reduce the manoeuvrability of advancing foot soldiers. I stopped once when my signaller thought he had raised Gough, but it was a false alarm.

Presently, on the southern road east of Oosterbeek, I caught up with the rear elements of Frost's battalion. They were moving in single file staggered along each side of the road, and moving very slowly. Farther on, others were halted. Frost was not at his HQ; he had gone ahead because some of his leading elements had run into trouble. I tried to impart a sense of urgency, which I hoped would be conveyed to Frost, and told them about the ill-fortune of the Recce Squadron.

Even so, I knew that Frost of all people would press on rapidly if it were humanly possible: a six-footer with an anxious moon face and permanent worry lines across his forehead, he relished a fight and had become one of the most capable battalion commanders in airborne forces. He had been in at the formation of the 2nd Battalion in the winter of 1941, and had subsequently led it with verve and distinction. In the historic Bruneval raid, he commanded the force built around a company of the 2nd Battalion in the attack on a radar station. Dropped from the air and evacuated by sea, they brought back with them secret equipment for examination and destroyed the remainder. All except eight men had got out to the waiting landing craft. Frost won the MC. He collected a DSO during the North African campaign and commanded the 2nd Battalion in the invasion of Sicily.

Despite a deceptive slow-motion air, Frost had developed a very fine tactical sense. As I talked with some of his officers, he was personally taking action to clear the blockage. It was the third occasion to date that they had dealt with opposition. First, the Germans had opened fire on them from the high ground near Heveadorp. Several men were lost. There had been a slight argument west of Oosterbeek, and now the leading men were trying to cope with an armoured-car which opened fire whenever they tried to make ground. An anti-tank gun was placed in a shop window ready for the next appearance of the armoured-car, while the parachutists slipped round the back of the houses. In the ensuing fight, a number of SS men were captured, and Frost came into possession of a German map giving the patrol route of an enemy recce unit. This indicated that the battalion's flanks and rear were menaced, and he had to take counter-measures.

It was obvious that Frost was now some way ahead on this winding cobbled road, and I therefore decided not to wait for him but to seek Gerald Lathbury. He had gone up to the 3rd Battalion on the middle road into Arnhem, in order to see how they were getting on. I had to return some way along the southern road, and someone reminded me of a somewhat hazardous stretch of about a hundred yards which was in full view of the Germans on the far bank of the river. On the way down, I had been aware of one or two bullets pinging past in this area. It seemed that there were German snipers high on the brickworks on the south bank, and they were taking pot-shots at anything that moved along the exposed bit of road. I was doing about 40 mph when we re-entered the gauntlet run, and stepped it up as much as I could in order to make myself a difficult target. At the bottom of the gradient with its dun-coloured setts the road narrowed and turned under a low bridge.

I turned right for the climb to the middle road. My signaller continued in his efforts to raise Gough. Two more parties of German prisoners under lone guards went past, and then we came upon the rear elements of the 3rd Battalion. A subaltern explained that Lathbury was up nearer the front. Within a few minutes I found the HQ halted at a major junction on the Arnhem–Utrecht highway. Almost on the corner was a Citroen staff car in the heavy, dull camouflage of the Wehrmacht: its windows were shattered, its tyres flattened. The door hung open revealing the body of a senior German officer who, it turned out, was Major-General Kussin, Field Commandant of Arnhem. Nearby lay the bodies of his interpreter, his batman and the driver.

I drove to the Arnhem side of the crossing and parked the jeep on the ride between the lines of trees. I could now hear the plop and whine of mortars, and some of these bombs were falling with unsettling accuracy on the crossroads and in the woodland where many of the 3rd Battalion men were under cover at the south-west corner of the junction. Medical orderlies were busy, and the shouts from the wood indicated that men were being hit and wounded by tree bursts. When Lathbury came up, I mentioned my suspicion that the

Germans probably had an observation post in one of the nearby villas, and suggested that a party might be sent to winkle it out. It occurred to neither of us at this moment that this was a bad place to pause. In retrospect, I think it is unlikely that the Germans needed an observation post; with typical Teuton thoroughness they had assumed our line of advance and had accurately ranged their mortars on this important crossroads from some 2000 yards away.

This was the first real evidence to come my way of the speed and determination of the German reaction; yet there was nothing to indicate that it was anything more than a local delaying action, and I was more impatient than anxious. In fact, although I was not to learn about it for a long time afterwards, the Germans had recovered from the initial surprise with extraordinary spirit and alacrity. In and around Arnhem and Oosterbeek that day were some 6000 German troops of mixed quality, ranging from the battle-hardened SS Grenadiers of the 9th and 10th Panzer Divisions and the 425 corporals at the SS school to those 'ear and stomach' battalions whose existence led some Allied intelligence staffs into loose thinking. For a change, the SS men had been taking things easy and on this quiet lazy day many had gone for walks and some had taken out their cycles to explore the woods north of the town. Discipline had been relaxed temporarily.

The SS major riding a cycle looted from France had set out for the open country. Presently, he heard the throb of aircraft and the crunch of flak and, pausing to stare upwards, he saw the sky filling with gliders and parachutes. One aircraft appeared to have been hit by the flak battery stationed at Arnhem Bridge. The major felt a twinge of surprise at this, for the bridge battery had an unenviable reputation as the worst in the entire Command.

Instead of continuing towards the country, which now was receiving other visitors, the major understandably turned round and pushed the pedals as hard as he could. He had been going only a few moments when a convoy of staff cars with their engines racing came from behind. Brakes shrieked and the leading car pulled up alongside. From the nearside front seat a plump and harassed Field-Marshal in a smart leather jacket leaned out and called: 'Which is the way to General Bittrich's headquarters?'

The major saluted and gave them directions to Doetinchem, and only then realized that the inquirer was Field-Marshal Model. Only by minutes had the commander of Army Group B avoided capture. He and his staff had been in such a hurry to leave their HQ at the Hartenstein and Taffelberg Hotels in Oosterbeek, which we were presently to know well, that one of Model's cases had burst open on the steps of his hotel, spilling out his spare underwear. Some of his officers had no time even to collect their personal possessions which were left along with a number of top secret documents. The major cycled into Arnhem to find confusion among the German troops: he was just in time to jump into a staff car bound for Bittrich's HQ. All over the town, small groups of Germans put themselves temporarily under the command of junior officers and NCOs, and, using cycles, horse-drawn carts, and wood-burning lorries, headed for the landing areas which were vaguely understood to be 'north of the town'. The HQ of the Panzer Corps swarmed with officers attempting to get troops on the move by contacting units on the public telephone system. They had lost much of their wireless gear in Normandy and now had to rely on the Dutch operators at the Arnhem switchboard, who gave them the worst possible service. Soldiers were sent out on cycles to convey orders.

The first Bittrich knew of the invasion was a report from a Luftwaffe listening post that landings were taking place, and soon afterwards he heard from the same source that large forces had landed at Arnhem and Nijmegen. He then ordered the Hohenstaufen Division (the 9th SS) to reconnoitre towards Arnhem and Nijmegen, and also to occupy Arnhem and 'defeat the troops west of Arnhem'. The Frundsberg Division (the 10th SS) was to be regrouped immediately – part of this division had begun a move into Germany for refit – and marched to Nijmegen. During the afternoon, as the defence took on some semblance of order with the appearance of SP guns and artillery, Bittrich dispatched a recce battalion of the 9th SS across the Arnhem Bridge to Nijmegen to hold the Americans there. It has been said that Bittrich displayed immense foresight in this move, for this battalion helped to repel the first tentative American thrust at the Nijmegen Bridge. Clearly, Bittrich had assumed from the start that our relief would have to come along the main road through Nijmegen from the 2nd Army, and was closing the route and hoping to dispose of us in detail. By this time, however, little perspicacity was needed by the German commanders in their counter-planning. Two hours after the landings had begun, the complete orders for the entire Airborne Corps operation were on the desk of General Student in his cottage at Vught. They had been found on the body of an American soldier in a glider shot down close to the village.

Thus, the carelessness or wilful disobedience of one soldier gave the Germans an immediate compensation for the advantage we had of surprise.

Student, with a widespread command incorporating the defence line against the 2nd Army and the battle against the 101st American Division, promptly passed on the information contained in the orders. At any rate, Bittrich in the late afternoon told one of his staff officers: 'The British intend to bridge all the gaps between their front line and the Reich.' He appeared to be under some strain as he ordered the recce battalion of the 9th SS south across the river. He was sending one of his crack units, and he confided to those nearest to him that he was banking on 'the British attack being not too daring and not too widespread'. Bittrich held some notions about the character and habits of the British Army which he now began to put into practice. 'We must remember,' he said, taking a breath of fresh air outside his HQ, 'that the British soldier will not act on his own initiative when he is fighting in the town and it becomes more difficult for officers to exercise control. He will be incredible in defence, but we need not be afraid of his offensive capabilities.' As he talked, he cast an occasional glance towards the battle area. It became clear that he was building his defence on the theory that the men of the 1st Airborne Division would attack only in places to which they had been specifically directed. These places would soon

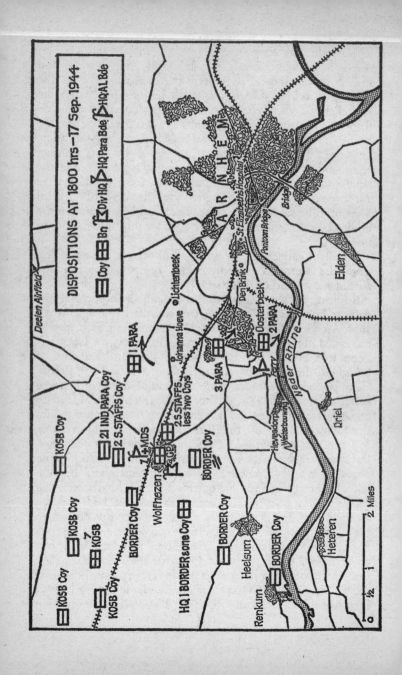

become obvious, and until reinforcements arrived from Army Group B, the Germans at Arnhem could afford to neglect the areas where we were not attacking.

It was a bold and daring conception.

But already John Frost and the 2nd Battalion were well on the way to causing General der Waffen SS Willi Bittrich some searching moments. By now, they were breaking into the town. Having disposed of the armoured-car obstacle, C Company of the 2nd Battalion had been sent by Frost to snatch the railway bridge west of the main target, the road bridge, and had moved across the exposed polder under cover of their own Brens. Just as Lieutenant Berry reached the bridge and some of his men were already on it, one of the spans was blown by the Germans. 'It seemed to curl back in our faces,' one of the men reported. Yet there were no casualties. C. Company then set out on its secondary task – the capture of the German HQ in Arnhem. Another company, B, had been sent to deal with the intervening Germans on the high ground at Den Brink. With A Company and his HQ personnel, Frost began a dash through the town, which was suddenly wide open to them.

At a few minutes before eight o'clock that evening, Frost and his men strained their eyes through the settling dusk and saw the towering outline of the great Bridge's span. It was intact. Stealthily, they moved closer and saw that German transport was still moving across – southwards.

The paratroopers tried to contain their excitement.

I knew nothing of Frost's success until much later. At the junction on the Arnhem–Utrecht road, the German mortar fire increased. There were some convenient slit trenches dug by the Germans on some earlier exercise. Lathbury told me of the opposition directly ahead. We discussed the slow rate of progress, and the difficulties presented by the high wire-mesh fencing the Dutch use as fences around their houses: it made outflanking an awkward business. A characteristic of the British soldier I had seen in other battles was his respect for the property and the houses of the people over whose land he fights. In ordinary circumstances, such civility would be a creditable thing. Now, I saw it as a time-waster. I was told that they were even knocking on doors and asking permission to search a house. They soon lost this politeness. We ducked as another mortar stonk straddled the wood and crossroads and I saw the second-in-command of one of the companies, Captain Thessiger, go down with a bad stomach wound. The Germans were making it hotter.

I was still feeling handicapped by the disappearance of Freddie Gough. Lathbury was also unhappy about the way the battle was developing at brigade level: he was completely out of touch with the 1st Battalion, which was presumably moving along to the north, and had established only intermittent contact with the 2nd Battalion. 'I'll get them off this crossroads first,' he said, and left me to return to my jeep to call Divisional HQ. As I approached, I saw that my jeep had been struck by a mortar. My signaller was badly wounded and was being removed by stretcher-bearers. The rover set was intact, but was clearly not working properly. I failed to make contact and so did Lathbury on his set.

Now I realized that I was losing control by being away from my own HQ. I was dissuaded from returning as this would have meant passing through areas which were not now in our hands. After some searching moments, I decided that at least I was now with the brigade charged with the initial thrust on the Bridge and thereby usefully placed to give on-the-spot instructions. I cursed the appalling communications. Furthermore, there was no reason to think they might be any better at Divisional HQ.

In the gathering dusk we made slow headway along the main road. Reports from in front were discouraging: the leading company was in contact with the enemy, and being held, close to the Hartenstein Hotel, on the outskirts of Oosterbeek. Despite the frustrating delays, the fact that I was up with the battle compensated to a certain extent for my inability to return to my Divisional HQ. Pip Hicks's Airlanding Brigade would have to remain around the dropping zones as protection for the arrival of Shan Hackett and the 4th Parachute Brigade tomorrow. The situation certainly didn't call for any reorientation which would have left the dropping zone unprotected.

Nevertheless, I wished I knew more of what was going on elsewhere. Just at the time when Frost and his men were moving stealthily into the houses and warehouses on the north side of the Bridge, we now paused. Darkness had fallen, and we were making little progress, and Lathbury, after a discussion with Fitch, the battalion commander, called a halt.

Patrols were pushed out towards the town, and we moved into a large villa set in a deep garden with well-kept lawns. The HQ personnel spread themselves through the house to which we were made welcome by a tall, middle-aged Dutchman with greying hair and solemn, honest eyes. I apologized for inconveniencing him and his wife, but he shrugged off our concern in remarkably good English. 'Not at all,' he said. 'It is worth anything to have *them* out.' He pointed downwards. 'And we are used to sleeping in the cellar. The RAF, you know. . . .' Lathbury and I shared the ground floor front room facing the road. We consumed some of our emergency rations, including a highly potent concentrate which became porridge on contact with water.

Outside, there was very little firing now.

Not far down the road, unknown to us, the troops of Reserve Battalion 16 who had been stationed in Oosterbeek and who had done more than any other Germans to delay us, were just being joined by the battle group 'Spindler' from the 9th SS Panzer Division. This must have been encouraging for the redoubtable commander of Battalion 16, Sturmbannführer Sepp Krafft: his defence of the Wolfhezen-Oosterbeek area had been costly. Earlier, he had said: 'The only way to draw the teeth of an airborne landing with an inferior force is to drive right into it.' This he had virtually done. One company had moved into the attack while the rest of the battalion had formed a defence line. Krafft had collected every tank and self-propelled gun he could get.

Up to now, he had been our most troublesome enemy. His battalion, which consisted of thirteen officers, seventy-three NCOs and 349 other ranks, made the most of country which was favourable to defence and put up resistance out of all proportion to their numbers. Major-General Kussin, whose body I had seen at one of the crossroads, had been returning from a visit to the battalion when his car was intercepted. Krafft had suggested that he should go back by a different route, but Kussin would not be put off.

During the afternoon, Krafft had been told by his Divisional HQ that another battalion would attack us from the north at eight o'clock. This had not materialized and he reported 'heavy casualties from a counter-attack by a heavily reinforced enemy'. He knew by this time of the movement of the 2nd Battalion along the southern road, and he also feared that his own battalion was in danger of being surrounded.

His anxieties were now momentarily relieved by the appearance of the 9th SS Panzer Division armour.

I dozed fitfully on a settee with my legs over one of the arm rests. Every now and then there were the usual HQ night sounds: motor-cycles, the crunch of boots on gravel, the disembodied conversations. I rose several times to check whether any signal had arrived from my HQ or from Gough, or from Frost whose arrival at the Bridge was still unknown to me.

In fact, Gough had just linked up with Frost at the Bridge approaches. Lacking most of its transport, his Recce Squadron had set out much later than the scheduled time. The leading jeeps were ambushed in the thick woods east of Wolfhezen Station and later the bodies of the crews were found. They had been machine-gunned. The whole squadron had got involved in a running fight along the edge of the wide railway track. They took some prisoners who yielded the information that the opposition came from the Training Battalion Krafft, which had arrived in the area only the day before.

The trainees fought furiously.

Gough withdrew under cover supplied by the 1st Battalion, which had also been held up. He attempted to get a message through to Lathbury to explain what had kept him, but the wireless failed. Accompanied by Pip Hicks, Gough made for Divisional HQ where Charles Mackenzie explained that I wanted him urgently.

'Where is he now?' Gough asked.

'With Lathbury,' Mackenzie replied.

58

Gough then suggested that his unit would still be useful at the Bridge, especially as he had with him a number of trained sappers who might be needed to clear the demolition charges the Germans had presumably laid.

'The Divisional commander was very insistent about seeing you,' Mackenzie persevered.

Taking an extra jeepload of Recce men for support, Gough then set off to find me. Five men to a jeep, they drove fast towards the middle road and came across the commander of the 3rd Light Battery, Major Dennis Mumford. 'No good continuing along here,' he warned. 'It's thick with Germans. Better get out quick.' The two jeeps turned round and detoured via the Renkum crossroads and, under the impression that Lathbury's HQ was intact and that it had linked up with the 2nd Battalion on the southern road, Gough speeded through the murk. It was after half past six when they reached that part of the 1st Brigade HQ on the riverside road and were informed that Lathbury and I had gone off with the 3rd Battalion and had not been heard of since.

'Do you know what I was wanted for?' Gough demanded.

'He wanted you to bring your unit along this road to follow Frost,' replied the brigade major, Tony Hibbert.

Again Gough tried to raise Divisional HQ on the radio, failed, and thereupon decided that he should press on and contact Frost.

At the Bridge, Frost seized the high buildings commanding a view along the girders, and was astonished at the lack of enemy reaction. In fact, if he had arrived only half an hour earlier he would have found the great prize absolutely unguarded. Some two dozen ageing veterans of the Wehrmacht had bolted at the first sign of trouble. Now, however, a group of SS men moved into position at the southern end. Looking out of an upper window of a house at the end of Markt Straat, Frost had a commanding view of the Bridge. In the darkened and quiet street he discerned a figure in some sort of uniform. It occurred to Frost that the man might be connected with the Resistance movement and he sent a parachutist to find out. After a minute or two, the soldier came back.

'Well?' Frost demanded.

'Oh, he's not Resistance, sir,' came the casual reply. 'He says he's Panzer SS.'

Frost had to turn away to bottle up his laughter.

And now he applied his thoughts to ways and means of taking the southern end of the Bridge.

As he was working out the next moves, Frost saw Gough and his party arrive. Gough once more tried to speak to me over the air but failed; then he familiarized himself with the layout of Frost's force, some of which was now in position in a school on the far side of the Bridge approach. Another section, under a likely major named Digby Tatham-Warter, was almost under the Bridge supports. Gough moved into a waterworks building with a high flat roof some fifty yards from the Bridge and commanding a view along the Bridge.

Frost had a lot to do. He sent an officer to try to get through to Lathbury, whose main HQ was now with the 2nd Battalion at the Bridge. With a party of sappers and a RASC platoon which had also come through, Frost now had some five hundred men spread around the perimeter of houses. In the dark, Lieutenant McDermont and a handful of men tried to rush across the Bridge only to be detected and driven back by combined fire from a pillbox and an armoured-car shooting straight along it. McDermont and Jack Grayburn were part of Tatham-Warter's party under the Bridge supports, and it was from this source that a further rush was attempted. Grayburn was hit and wounded.

Meanwhile, Frost had ordered B Company to take the south side of the Bridge by crossing the river in small boats which had been spotted floating in an inlet close to the site of the pontoon bridge which had been dismantled earlier by the Germans. At this stage, however, the company was still dealing with the opposition on the ridge at Den Brink and it wasn't until three o'clock in the morning that they were able to reach the site. An officer's patrol was sent to locate C Company at the German HQ in Arnhem. The patrol found the company surrounded and was unable to reach them.

Around the bridgehead, anti-tank guns were sited, mines were laid on the embankment leading to the Bridge and

Hawkins grenades on the approaches. In the top floors of warehouses and other buildings, such machine-guns as had arrived were sited. In one house, the paratroopers found a bedridden old woman, too old and too near to her natural end to be afraid. She was offended by their suggestion that they should evacuate her and insisted that she preferred to stay and see the Germans out. The soldiers began to take it in turns to look after her with food and hot drinks.

In the deceptive half light of this autumn evening, Frost, Gough and others could make out what appeared to be a series of wooden huts lining the western side of the Bridge. Each was about twenty feet in length. In front of them was the pillbox which had already given a good deal of trouble. Frost ordered that a way should be found of putting a flame-thrower on to it, and two sappers wriggled up the embankment with the weapon. As they got into position the sapper aiming the flame-thrower was about to fire when he was distracted by his companion with the result that the flame looped past the pillbox and struck the huts. A tremendous, blinding explosion lit and rocked the whole area. Houses shook and debris was scattered. In the houses the vigilant soldiers felt the pressure of the blast. It needed no expert to realize that the huts had been stacked with ammunition. And now tracer and small-arms fire and mortar bombs sparked off an accompaniment.

Shielding their eyes against the glare, Frost and Gough and several hundred others saw that part of the Bridge was blazing. 'Now that's a fine thing to come all this way for,' said one of his men to Gough.

Optimistically, Gough retorted: 'It's only the paintwork.' He hoped he was right.

During the evening, Frost had further reinforcements. As the 3rd Battalion had approached Oosterbeek, C Company under Major Lewis moved towards the railway in Arnhem with orders to find a route, any route, which led to the Bridge. After one short, sharp engagement, they had reached the heart of Arnhem at dusk and found themselves in a deserted town. From the railway station they moved cautiously through the narrow shopping streets, alert for snipers and not sure what they were going to find on arrival. Nobody tackled them until they entered the street leading to the Bridge, and there they were engaged after some members of the company had blown up a German armoured-car with a gammon bomb. On the way through the town, one of the soldiers had entered a butcher's shop in search of food. The shopkeeper appeared and apologized for being out of meat but offered him bread, cheese and a glass of wine and asked the paratrooper to remain while he brought his daughter to see this phenomenon from Britain.

The officer sent by Frost to contact Lathbury returned to the Bridge with the news that the Germans had now cut the southern road behind the battalion. Frost therefore ordered Gough to remain, and prepared to meet the counter-attacks he knew must be brewing. Already he had caused Bittrich to change his orders. While the recce battalion of the 9th SS had crossed the Bridge before Frost's arrival, the 10th SS Division was too late. Back at Doetinchem, Bittrich learned from a Wehrmacht telephonist that the Bridge had been taken by the British. He was concerned that we should be liquidated before the 2nd Army came through, and it was imperative that he should get the Frundsberg Division over the Neder Rhine. He now ordered it to cross the river by ferry at Huissen, and take over a bridgehead south of Nijmegen. Meanwhile, the Hohenstaufen Division was to recapture the Arnhem Bridge as soon as possible; prevent any reinforcement of the British party at the Bridge from Oosterbeek, and finally to surround and annihilate the 1st Airborne Division as soon as Wehrmacht reinforcements came from Model.

The Hohenstaufen Division consisted of one regiment of Panzergrenadiers, an artillery detachment, two batteries of heavy guns, an armoured reconnaissance unit, a tank company, and parts of a pioneer unit and a flak detachment. Most of these troops had been fighting as infantry throughout the day under a new commander who had temporarily taken over the division, an agile obersturmbannführer named Harzer.

Now the Frundsberg Division began to cross by the ferry. At the Bridge, Frost temporarily accepted the great steel span as No Man's Land. The paratroopers at the northern end, and the SS men at the southern, stared across towards each other, unable to see anything but the dying flames on the Bridge, the reflections in the water, and the vague grey shape of the towering steel arch.

From the house where we had paused for a few hours on the main Arnhem–Utrecht road, Gerald Lathbury sent a signal to Frost with the news that the rest of the 1st Brigade would not now attempt to reach the Bridge until morning. The 1st Battalion, like the 3rd which I was for the present accompanying, had run into some spasmodic but fierce fighting. Led by Lieutenant-Colonel David Dobie it had made an encouraging start along the Arnhem–Ede road. Dutch civilians had showered the men with greetings and affection and, as the result of a previous strafing of German positions and flak points ahead of them, the troops made rapid headway. To the south, they heard the sounds of battle; but it was not until late in the afternoon that they caught sight of German tanks – old models, but sufficiently menacing to keep the troops alive to the potential trouble ahead. As darkness fell one company moved into a wood where it was engaged almost immediately. In the lane, a Piat opened fire on a German armoured-car which was scouting the area. This was followed by a force of five tanks and fifteen half-tracks. As the 1st Battalion engaged these, they were shot at by Germans who had closed in behind them. After midnight, the battalion moved through the woods, and before dawn was entering the outskirts of Arnhem. Casualties were high: R Company, which had been sharply engaged at a road junction north of Wolfhezen earlier on, had now suffered more losses through mortar fire in the woods and was only at half strength. Another company had had thirty casualties. And now Dobie's signallers picked up a call from Frost at the Bridge requesting urgent reinforcements. He tried to contact Lathbury, and when the signals failed, he decided that the situation called for a departure from his original plan. Instead of persevering with his role of seizing and holding the high ground north of the town, he would turn south-east and make directly for the Bridge. This way he might be able to help Frost. Patrol information showed quite

63

clearly that the Germans were on the northern high ground in some strength and that any further bid to take it would have been costly, anyway.

At first light, Dobie's battalion started its advance. It was joined at this stage by the headquarters company of the 3rd Battalion, and moved on the suburb of Mariendaal where the enemy were dug in among the houses and at a factory close to a railway bridge. In costly and bloody fighting, Dobie made some ground. The smoke and smell of battle filled the morning air.

By now, I had heard something of 3rd Battalion's efforts before I had come up with them. Under Fitch, they had been engaged within an hour of setting off from the dropping zone in an area some two miles south-east of Wolfhezen. First, the leading platoon under a young captain with a fierce and spreading moustache had got off to a fast start. Jimmy Cleminson, of whom I was presently to see a great deal, had concussed himself slightly on landing and moved off with a soldier checking his map for him. They were already beyond a major crossroads on their way into Arnhem when they heard a car approaching from the road to their left. The brakes squealed as the driver noticed the parachutists and tried to stop and reverse. Even before the car stopped, it had been riddled from Stens, rifles and revolvers. Two men tried to break for it, and were killed. In the excitement, parachutists on both sides of the junction were firing at the car and Cleminson had to order them to stop it. He was concerned lest they should begin to disfigure each other. One minute earlier, and Major-General Kussin and his companions would have escaped.

The leading platoon continued for another quarter of an hour before encountering the enemy again. This time, a self-propelled gun was shooting straight down the road at them and, with Peter Waddy, his company commander, Cleminson worked out a plan. They each took a patrol to the right and left of the road and could make only painfully slow progress through the gardens because of the high, close-meshed fencing. Meanwhile, a six-pounder was brought up, but before its crew could swing it round, the self-propelled gun tracked down the road and put it out of action, killing some of the crew. The German gun then opened fire along the road. Waddy and Cleminson and their parties got into houses and attacked the vehicle with Brens and Stens. They were without anti-tank weapons except gammon bombs and the distance of the houses from the road made accurate throwing a difficult project. Nevertheless, several parachutists set themselves to hurl the bombs as the self-propelled gun came back past their positions. The German crew were able to run the gauntlet with some safety, however, for they took the precaution of picking up one of the wounded British anti-tank gunners and laying him across the front of their vehicle.

The self-propelled gun departed.

Others were quickly on the scene, though, and as the hold-up developed, Fitch sent C Company down a side road to by-pass the opposition. This was the company which later had joined up with Frost at the Bridge.

It was still not dark on D-Day when Cleminson and his party reached the Hartenstein Hotel with its spacious lawns and comfortable atmosphere; an imposing, white rectangular building with tall windows and a woodland backcloth. The Hartenstein is set deep from the road and the parachutists suspiciously entered singly via the cellars and prepared for a winkling-out operation. Inside, they found all the signs of a hasty exit, a bar with some liquor and a range of glasses, and the first course of a luncheon laid out on the long mess table in the ground floor front room.

Cleminson and the others helped themselves to the *hors d'œuvre*. Some papers were found which were left for examination by Intelligence, and two officers tossed up for the duty of moving off first into the town. It was evident that there could be little reward in attempting further direct approaches along the main road in the face of the mobile and somewhat destructive self-propelled guns. 'We'll not get on fast enough if we keep to the road,' Waddy announced. He glanced at the map, and fingered a short cut due east through the parkland of the Arnhem side of the hotel.

Presently, the first party moved off, only to be spotted by

German machine-gunners. The approach was well-covered and Waddy and Cleminson dropped back to the Hartenstein. Unknown to them, C Company was at this moment getting through within hailing distance on their right. Farther back within the 3rd Battalion HQ, I was roused soon after 3 am in the villa. We took up the advance again on a different line. Fitch had decided to move on to the southern road through Oosterbeek. As I came out into the road, I found myself accompanied by a massive shape which turned out to be the 3rd Battalion's RSM, a six feet two inches Grenadier named Lord. 'From now on, sir,' he informed me, 'I'm your bodyguard.' Not even Generals like to admit that they need protection, and I gave some nonchalant response; nevertheless, I found his presence rather reassuring. Slowly, frustratingly so, we headed down the road; occasionally from in front came the sound of sharp encounters, brief bursts of fire which brought the entire column to a stop. I found these constant delays most wearing, and although I conveyed my feelings to Lathbury, there was little either of us could do about it. Some of the men up front were very young and had not experienced action before; others had not been in battle since the campaigns in North Africa and Sicily. I knew that in such circumstances it was inevitable that they would stop sometimes unnecessarily and pay too much attention to the odd bullet, as soldiers do in the early stages of any fight. In an airborne attack, this factor must be minimized if full benefit is to be reaped from the advantage of surprise. I have many times gone over in my mind the reasons for the Battle of Arnhem going the way it did, the mistakes and misjudgments and inadequacies. It is possible that less respect by the troops in the early stages for the German opposition would have allowed us to get more men to the Bridge, though it is doubtful if this would have made much difference to the ultimate outcome and might well have involved a longer casualty list.

Anyhow, the caution of the troops newly under fire or coming into it after a long lay-off was instinctive; furthermore, as a divisional commander mixed up in a battalion encounter, and personally situated somewhere in the middle of the column at that, I was in the worst possible position to intervene too much.

Even after we left the main road on the new diversion, the stops were no less frequent. As daylight came, we were still jinking about the side roads of the western approach to Arnhem. The local people, who offered us great encouragement and later practical help, came into the streets bearing fruit and drinks for the rear companies of passing soldiers. Orange coloured armbands and favours were in evidence and had obviously been carefully set aside for just such an occasion as this. Even the children were out in force, marching imitatively alongside the paratroopers, thrilled by the pats on the head and the bars of milk chocolate. In some cases, housewives came out with pots of steaming ersatz coffee: it was a most precious commodity at this time in Holland.

All this was very impressive and moving, but I was conscious of the precious seconds it was costing in view of the need for a rapid follow-through to the Bridge and for the securing of established positions by the time Shan Hackett's 4th Parachute Brigade were dropped later in the morning. Soon, this second lift would free Hicks's Airlanding Brigade to come up with us.

As we reached the lower road, it was apparent that the 2nd Battalion must have gone through, and soon we had confirmation of this when we picked up the rear company of the 2nd Battalion which had become separated from the main body. We made good headway and then, on the sweeping bend just west of the St Elizabeth Hospital where the lower road again joined the main road, the Germans halted our leading elements. They were shooting down the road, and they had brought up some self-propelled guns and a few tanks which wheezed and rattled around the district with extra sheets of armour plate hanging loose like metal skirts to reinforce the basic armour. By now, Cleminson and the leading company were cut off from the rest of us physically and even by wireless. They kept going until they reached a riverside building known as the Rhine Pavilion where the Germans fought with grimness and hit several of the advancing parachutists. One party took a route through the wood overlooking the Pavilion and vanished. Waddy caught up with Cleminson and explained that as they were out of touch with the battalion it would be advisable to fall back up the hill and to the left behind St Elizabeth Hospital, a spreading building surrounded by low walls and railings.

Even as he spoke, the little spearhead force came under heavy attack. The survivors spread themselves among the houses along the main road.

As we had now struck substantial German opposition I moved with Lathbury a few yards off the road into a three-storeyed house which had a flat roof on the first floor level at the rear. Later, an obsolete tank rattled down the main road and the parachutists of the 3rd Battalion, timing it nicely, stopped the thing with plastic grenades; handfuls of explosive which they were adept at using. We were now stuck. Soon, the Germans had located us and the mortar bombs came down behind the roadside houses in which we had taken temporary cover. As other tanks and self-propelled guns made their appearance in the road at the front, so there developed an exchange of small-arms shooting between the houses at the rear. Looking through one of the back windows I saw that we were in a thickly built-up part of the town: there were rows of terraced houses divided by a maze of gardens fenced and walled off in the usual thorough Dutch style. There was a good deal of small-arms fire across this area and I was told that there were Germans in the upper rooms of the houses across the gardens.

My prospects of returning to Divisional HQ appeared for the present more remote than I would have liked.

# CHAPTER THREE

OUR SITUATION quickly took on the appearances of a siege. On the rear balcony of the house, chairs and other furniture were stacked to make a firing point and from behind this makeshift barrier and from the upper windows parachutists knelt to fire into the houses across the allotments. I saw Lathbury lying there and taking pot-shots with a rifle. Presently, the battalion commander, Fitch, joined us for a spell and junior officers, very young and terribly solicitous about our welfare, called with bits of information and also to see how were were making out.

In the front road a Mark IV tank came into view and Major Waddy with great deliberation and accuracy stopped it with a gammon bomb thrown from the house next door to ours. This caused some good-natured expressions of envy in our house, where others had lain in wait ready to hurl their bombs. Tanks were top prizes. Two of them now lay knocked out in the road without, however, preventing movement of other armoured vehicles which were now more brazenly trundling up and down the road as a preliminary to blasting us out. Amid this German monopoly of mobility, however, there suddenly appeared a Bren carrier, its engine roaring, its tracks clattering on the small setts. It was driven by a ubiquitous Canadian lieutenant called Heaps who was soon to develop a reputation for turning up in the most unlikely places at the most unexpected times with his Bren carrier. In fact, I never really discovered to which unit he belonged. In battle, some men have charmed existences: Heaps was such a man. He took unto himself the role of mobile freelance. On this occasion, he had with him in the carrier a lean and cadaverous civilian standing six feet three or four inches. I noted his orange armband which marked him as one of the Dutch people who were out to help us in this operation: he was in fact a Resistance leader named Labouchere.

Heaps saluted and brought tidings from my own HQ which were far from encouraging. Things were not going well. The second lift had been delayed, and the communications failure, as we well knew, was preventing a co-ordinated effort. 'You were reported missing,' he told me. 'I was sent to try and find you and bring back information.'

I gave him a message for Mackenzie at my HQ telling him what was happening around me and asking him to try to organize some further help for Frost's 2nd Battalion at the Bridge. I visualized that Frost must now be getting very short of ammunition, particularly of the anti-tank variety such as Piat bombs, for I imagined that he was meeting the same kind of resistance that we were experiencing – and probably much more intense.

Heaps and Labouchere returned to the carrier and despite German attempts to stop them, managed to set off back along the road.

After I had left my HQ the day before, Mackenzie had grown increasingly alarmed at my absence. My ADC, Graham Roberts, suggested going to look for me. There were rumours that I had been killed, wounded, taken prisoner. During the evening the HQ came in for desultory mortaring which convinced Mackenzie that it was not the best place to spend the night. He ordered a move back to the landing zone and at dusk they set themselves up in some deserted gliders. Frequently in the night Mackenzie inquired for news of my whereabouts to no avail, and before first light the HQ moved again, this time into a group of houses bordering the wood on the Heelsum road. By 9 am on Monday, Mackenzie had made a number of minor decisions in consort with Robert Loder-Symonds, the chief gunner, including one affecting the Border Regiment positions near the river at Renkum on the extreme west of our area. He knew now that Frost had reached the Bridge and that a major decision was needed in order to boost the support effort required to reinforce the Bridge party.

Mackenzie pondered on the situation a moment and then, turning to Loder-Symonds, remarked: 'The only one with any chaps is Hicks. We can't order him to deflect part of his strength. But the time has perhaps come when he ought to come here and order himself to do it.' Mackenzie then explained to Loder-Symonds the chain of command instruction I had given him before the battle – Lathbury, Hicks, Hackett.

Loder-Symonds concurred and the two lieutenant-colonels set off by jeep to find Hicks. They met him on a dusty cart track close by a copse and there Mackenzie explained the position. Hicks thereupon made arrangements for his second-in-command, Hilary Barlow, to take over the brigade and returned with the two officers. They arrived at Divisional HQ at 9.15 am. Hicks familiarized himself as best as he could with the situation and then ordered one of the landing zone protection units, the 2nd Battalion South Staffords, to move off and assist the drive for the Bridge.

By now, the Germans who were pinning us in the houses alongside the road near the hospital had resumed their attacks. It must have been obvious to them that we had not unlimited supplies of ammunition and the tanks and self-propelled guns became progressively more impertinent. I was concerned also about the intermittent shooting at the rear, and more than once wondered whether the snipers in the houses across the allotments might be other members of the 1st Parachute Brigade and not Germans. The attack had become so disjointed that this was a fair possibility in view of the fact that the 1st Battalion had been north of us. I have since studied this particular incident closely, and I am today convinced that in fact there *was* inter-British shooting and that those houses contained elements of the 1st Battalion.

The Germans were in positions close to the hospital and on the higher ground beyond the line of houses from which we were being shot at. Just as there had been so much nervous shooting at shadows in the early hours, so now there was a good deal of indiscriminate firing across the allotments. We had a number of wounded in the houses now, and outside lay the bodies of several paratroopers. It was clear now that the main road was inhospitable, and we knew it would be unhealthy to move out towards the lower road where earlier parties had been given a hot reception. On his own initiative, Major Waddy set off to reconnoitre the back street approaches on the north side of our position. I saw him go down the steps of the house, wondering what he was about; then, as he was crossing the small square of lawn, a mortar exploded and he fell. He was the only soldier I ever saw killed solely by blast and when they picked him up there was not a single mark on him. He was buried in the garden where he had fallen.

Later, as the casualties mounted, there seemed to be no future in staying where we were and if we were to get the battle moving again we had to take a chance on following the route which Waddy had had in mind. 'We must get on,' I said to Lathbury. 'We'll have to try and break out.'

'I agree,' he said. 'Our best prospect seems to be to get out the back way and push on into the town where presumably the rest of the Brigade are now involved.'

Looking outside, I was pleased to see the fine and sunny conditions which augured well for the arrival of the 4th Parachute Brigade. From the front of the house came the sound of an explosion and I guessed that the men out there had put paid to another self-propelled gun. As we went downstairs towards the back door, Lathbury turned and I saw that his normally serious face was creased with a mischievous smile. Already the parachutists had started to cover our movements with smoke bombs and Lathbury remarked: 'Would you like to throw a bomb, sir?'

'No,' I replied, 'you are much better at it than I am.'

I came out of the back door and was striking over the fence, with Lathbury alongside, when his Sten went off. The shot narrowly missed my right foot. I chided him about soldiers who could not keep their Stens under control. It was bad enough for a divisional commander to be jinking about in what was now hardly more than a company action, and it would have been too ironic for words to be laid low by a bullet fired by one of my brigadiers.

Lathbury regarded his Sten with disgruntled concern. 'I'm awfully sorry,' he said. 'A temperamental weapon at best.'

Beyond the fence, in the lee of the row of houses, a Dutchman came out to offer us a jug of ersatz coffee – bitter, foul-tasting stuff which we accepted and drank rather than offend him. After all, most of his neighbours had sensibly taken to the cellars during the battle. We thanked him, and made our way across a small garden past the lone tree to the feet of a ten-feet-high brick wall. With one man astride the top giving a hand to others, the party went over one by one. Someone gave me a push and I got my hands over the top but my boots could get no purchase in the crumbling plaster. I came back to earth and tried again. I felt a heave from behind and I was over. On the far side a short path beyond a wire fence led into a narrow arched passageway between the houses. We ran through the passageway, where our studded boots made a tremendous echoing noise, and out into a narrow, cobbled street. Two officers had gone ahead of us. And now, as we ventured out, one of them called a warning. He had seen us turn right, in the direction of St Elizabeth Hospital at the end of the street, where he knew there were Germans; but we failed to hear him. Summoning others, he came after us.

Now there were four of us running along this street which had intersections on the left side every twenty yards. As we passed the first of these, a Spandau opened fire from the top end. We ran on, and as we passed the second inter-section Lathbury was hit by a burst and fell. The two young officers and myself managed to lift him past the street corner into a terrace house, 135 Alexander Straat, where an astonished Dutch couple in early middle-age watched us in silence. We laid Lathbury on the floor and a quick examination revealed that he was not dangerously wounded; he had been partially paralysed by a bullet which had snicked his spine. He was bleeding but still conscious. All of us knew he could travel no farther. The Germans knew roughly where we were and it would be senseless to try and take them on. As if he knew what we were thinking, Lathbury urged: 'You must leave me. It's no use staying. You'll only get cut off.'

I turned to the two officers, one of whom was Jimmy Cleminson, who had shouted the unheeded warning a few moments earlier, and the other a boyish-looking intelligence officer on Lathbury's HQ called Taylor, and said: 'We must try and get some proper medical attention for him.' At that moment I spotted a German soldier as he appeared at the window. I had an automatic in my hand and fired point-blank at a range of a few feet; the window shattered and the German dropped outside.

The Dutch couple now reappeared. They had been talking things over and, realizing our plight, they now contrived to make us understand that they would take care of Lathbury and have him taken across the road into the hospital as soon as possible. In order to afford him protection from any other inquisitive German who might peer in at the window, we moved Lathbury into a space under the stairs at the top of the cellar steps, and said our farewells. Convinced that we would be taken on, we were ready for a fight when we slipped out of the back door into yet another maze of tiny, fenced gardens. We crossed these, turned right then left into another terrace house set at right angles to the one we had left. Our entry through the kitchen of 14 Zwarteweg came as a shock to Anton Derksen and family. A plump and solemn Dutchman, he pointed to the stairs just behind the door. In Dutch he tried to tell us that the Germans were already coming round the corner. I found the stairs almost too narrow for my boots, and the ceiling low for a six-footer. On the landing we paused before entering a bedroom with a single wooden bed under the window. I glanced down into the street and saw the familiar field-grey uniforms of the Wehrmacht. Opposite was the hospital.

Cleminson took a look and then said: 'We can't get out this way. The place is crawling with 'em.'

Taylor had made a cautionary inspection at the back. 'Can we be sure of these people?' he asked, nodding in the direction of the stairs. 'There's an open attic over this room from which we might keep the entrance in view.' It was not much more than a deep shelf shaped by the slope of the roof and the bedroom ceiling. As we discussed the next move, a self-propelled gun whined to a stop almost right underneath our window. We climbed the detachable steps to the shelf, pulled them up after us, and waited. We had pistols, and we now primed our hand grenades. I had two in my blouse which I had almost forgotten about.

'Funny nobody followed us up,' Cleminson observed.

We watched the stairs.

There was no sign of any of the family we had seen on arrival. We hoped that they and their neighbours could be relied upon not to give us away, and if we had then known more about these people we would have been less troubled in mind. In those moments we expected the Germans to burst in at any time. The house remained still and silent and we could not even hear the family downstairs. I brought out a bag of sweets and a bar of chocolate Hancock had given me in exchange for my cigarettes. Outside, we could hear German voices, and occasionally from farther away, bursts of fire. We settled back, and hoped that the commotion would die down. I was suddenly struck by the size of Cleminson's moustache, one to make the RAF envious. This enormity in hirsute handlebars had earlier been lost on me but now there was little else to look at. On such a slightly built man they looked weird.

Presently, when it became obvious that the Germans did not know our whereabouts, the idiocy of the situation forced itself upon me. 'I think it's time we tried to get out,' I said. 'I don't know how you chaps feel, but we are less than useless cooped up here.' I felt that as a divisional commander I ought not to be indulging in such frolics of evasion.

'I don't think it's going to be that easy yet,' said Cleminson, 'but we can take a look.'

Taylor lowered the ladder and crossed into the bedroom to check on the street. As Cleminson and I joined him, he remarked: 'They're down there still, the SP crew.' Looking out of the window, I saw the German crew standing around only seven or eight yards away; some were smoking, others attending to spot maintenance on their vehicle.

Anything seemed better to me than to stay out of the battle in this way. There was no knowing what was happening to the division, and here was I, ineffective as a spectator and, in more senses than one, shelved. 'There's no future in this,' I suddenly announced. 'We're contributing nothing. We could lob a grenade on this thing down here and make a dash for it.' I saw that Taylor and Cleminson regarded this suggestion as more than slightly unworkable but my long

75

absence from the centre of affairs was uppermost in my mind.

It was a big risk that seemed worth the taking.

Taylor, a brisk young officer who looked more like a schoolboy, considered that we would do better to wait. I looked at Cleminson whose magnificent spread of whiskers failed to cover up his extreme youth, and said: 'All right. We'll have a majority decision on this.' I did not feel justified in ordering them to break out with me.

'Even if we knock out the gun and its crew, which we could do quite easily,' Cleminson said, 'we would be killed or caught. I'd prefer to wait for an attack to catch up with us rather than go prowling around.' I was outvoted.

There was neither food nor water in the house – the Germans had cut off supplies of water at the mains – and the lack of indoor sanitation was a nuisance. We hated having to soil this family's living quarters, and long afterwards when I sought out the family I apologized for our unavoidable behaviour.

Outside, there was a good deal of activity around the hospital and I wondered how much of it concerned our own casualties. I was frustrated at my inability to influence the battle, and the minutes dragged through the evening and night.

If I had known just how badly the battle was going elsewhere, I would certainly have attempted to reach my HQ. It is doubtful, however, if I could have succeeded.

In the early hours of Monday, Frost and his men at the Bridge had watched in tense fascination as three lorries loaded with Germans approached. The order to fire held back until the enemy were really between the British positions, and then the trucks were suddenly riddled with bullets and struck by gammon bombs. Only two Germans, both badly hurt, escaped. In a house to the left of Frost's HQ some of his men had a glorious view of the Bridge and its far approaches along the Nijmegen road and presently they reported that the Germans were accumulating a sizeable convoy and were presumably getting ready to rush the Bridge from the south. The convoy started to move. Behind the tall windows, and in attics and slit trenches, the parachutists again displayed astonishing aplomb as they waited for the exact moment.

The armoured column came on. When it was half way across the Bridge, it was evident that it consisted of armoured-cars and half-tracks. It came closer. Silently the parachutists waited, their fingers on the triggers. The convoy reached the northern end of the Bridge and the leading vehicles were on the approach – one, two, three, four. Those of Frost's men with the best view counted sixteen armoured vehicles. And now all hell was let loose as the gunners with their six-pounders, and Piat marksmen, and the machine-gunners caught them in the trap. It was successful. Six vehicles toppled over the embankment; others blazed, halted yet firing back; the few which survived the gauntlet were driven close to the parallel wings of the school occupied by the sappers. Corporal Simpson and Sapper Perry fired straight down into them with automatic weapons. One of the half-tracks was hit as it turned right by the school and its crew were killed as they dived for the bushes. In the midst of all this, Frost saw Gough, his face flushed and beaming, behind a machine-gun.

The Germans next tried to put infantry across the river but these attacks were broken by mortar fire from Frost's men and artillery bombardments called up from the gunners at Oosterbeek and directed by Mumford in an OP commanding the Bridge. Their fire was accurate enough to be of great encouragement to Frost. Not to be outdone in their determination to carry out Bittrich's order to retake the Bridge, the Germans now laid down an increasingly severe mortar and artillery attack. Frost's men were suffering casualties under this murderous fire. The Germans confidently sited a medium gun in the open and prepared it for use against the 2nd Battalion. Just as it was ready, the parachutists picked off the crew before it could fire a round. Then these men were forced to watch helplessly as the Germans sent out a Mark IV tank to retrieve the gun and tow it away.

Delighted as he was by the performance of his men in beating off all these German efforts to dislodge them from the Bridge – he had already described the smashing of the

German reconnaissance squadron as 'a lovely action' – Frost was nonetheless anxious for some sign of relief. His troops persistently asked for news. Now and then, above the din of their own action they heard sounds of fighting to the west. It appeared to be getting no nearer.

Then Frost made contact with Dobie, and urged that he should move with all speed. In order to try and help the 1st and 3rd Battalions Frost sent out a harassing party to take the Germans who were facing them, in the rear. This move had little effect because of the enemy's armoured strength: tanks and self-propelled guns patrolled the area in force now.

Late in the afternoon, the Germans tried to get into Frost's positions from the east along the river bank. They were driven off in some disorder when the parachutists, shouting their remarkable battle cry 'Whoa, Mohammed!' went in with fixed bayonets. In bitter house-to-house fighting which ensued a number of parachutists were killed. The positions were held. Some prisoners were taken in this and subsequent forays, and several were identified as belonging to the 9th and 10th SS Panzer Divisions – a revelation that caused Frost his first serious disquiet about the outcome. Under interrogation, these Panzergrenadiers yielded the information that they were part of the reforming panzer corps which had been collected in the Arnhem area. Frost realized ruefully that he could expect determined attacks from such élite troops. Even now, the two medical officers were being kept busy. And as darkness came down to herald the 2nd Battalion's second night at the Bridge, the little force was subjected to the heaviest stonk yet – from mortars and self-propelled guns and 20-mm and 40-mm guns which shattered a number of buildings and set others on fire. One shell blasted the room occupied by the little old lady the troops had found in one of the houses; when the men rushed upstairs they found she was dead.

Four houses blazed fiercely. It was a dry, almost cloudless evening and now a strong breeze came up from the north-east to fan the flames. Nothing the parachutists could do was enough to put out the fires. Out of the blazing houses men stumbled to take up other positions. The lurid, flickering glare played tricks and the snipers were sometimes shooting at men and sometimes only at reflections and smoke shadows. Many men died and others fought back and pulled wounded comrades out of trouble. An ancient German howitzer got a direct hit from one of the British mortar teams. One of the medical officers, Jimmy Logan, advised Father Egan, the padre with the party, that one young soldier had only a quarter of an hour to live. As Egan knelt by the youngster's side with words of comfort, he reckoned that the soldier could not be more than twenty years old.

'If you'll bring a couple of stretcher-bearers along, Padre,' the young man said quietly, 'I can handle a rifle. Just let them put me in position.'

Already in this battle, Egan had seen much gallantry. 'I'm sorry,' he said disarmingly, 'but the stretcher-bearers are too busy just now.'

Presently, the soldier was placated, but remarked: 'I only hope the others don't think I'm letting them down.'

Egan stayed with him until he died.

During another bombardment, Egan found himself sharing a house with a number of soldiers, one of whom remarked unoriginally: 'Well, Padre, they've thrown everything but the kitchen stove.' A moment later the room was showered with laths and plaster as the ceiling came down – with, incredibly, a cooker. As the dust was settling, and the last bits of masonry collapsed, the soldier surveyed his colleagues, who were picking themselves up, and then the wreckage, and said: 'I knew the bastards were close, but I didn't think they could hear us talking.'

There were other critical moments when the cheerful cynicism of the British soldier displayed itself. At one stage of the battle, a tough, squarely built captain named Panter discovered a quantity of German supplies including cigarettes. He gave them out to his men. As he moved among the soldiers, he overheard one of them say: 'The old bastard thinks he's Father Christmas!'

By Monday evening, the Germans were sufficiently inspired by the blaze in the battalion area to hurl in more incendiaries and at times there was close-quarter fighting among the houses.

Around 8 pm Frost made contact with Divisional HQ and again stressed the urgency of his position. He was heartened to hear that two battalions were to attempt a breakthrough during the night along with reserves of ammunition. It was the first intimation Frost had that the second lift had arrived. He had also been casting his eye hopefully on the road across the river leading to Nijmegen for signs of the spearhead of XXX Corps.

He looked in vain, for XXX Corps was still a long way off. Its leading tanks were waiting while sappers built a bridge over the Wilhelmina Canal at Zon. General Horrocks had relied on a single thrust up the main road through Eindhoven led by tanks and followed by other tank squadrons carrying infantry. With support from Typhoons of the 2nd Tactical Air Force the attack had got under way soon after 2.30 pm on Sunday and by dusk the Irish Guards had reached the day's objective, Valkenswaard, just south of Eindhoven. By Monday afternoon the Guards linked up with the 101st US Airborne Division in Eindhoven and moved forward to Zon.

At Nijmegen, Jim Gavin, commander of the 82nd US Airborne Division, had the job of seizing the great Nijmegen Bridge with its 570 yards span. He was also ordered to control the ridge of high ground from which the Germans, fighting from the Reichswald Forest, might prejudice the entire Allied operation. And of all his objectives, the ridge had priority. Stretching some twelve miles south of Nijmegen, and 300 feet high in places, the ridge, which is the highest ground in Holland, dominates the area around it. If securely held, it was a natural defence barrier to German counter-attacks from the Reichswald. Gavin knew that he had to keep possession of this ridge. He was nevertheless eager to take the main Nijmegen Bridge and to this end he dispatched a small force right at the start of the operation. And then, during Monday afternoon, he outlined to Boy Browning who had landed south of Nijmegen with his Corps HQ, a plan for seizing the bridge with two battalions of paratroopers attacking from east and west. At first Browning approved the idea, but after turning it over in his mind he decided that it was more important to retain the high ground.

At this point, XXX Corps and the 82nd Airborne Division had not linked up. Horrocks's XXX Corps was behind schedule.

Gavin called off his attack.

On all this, as well as on the efforts of the rest of our own division in Arnhem and Oosterbeek, Frost was depending for help. As night fell, and the air around the bridge was filled with the acrid smoke of fires, and explosives, and the stench of battle, no news of the delay had reached Frost.

He still expected to be relieved.

Meanwhile, things could hardly have been worse for Hicks from the moment he took over command of the division in my absence. Lacking reliable information about the dispositions and activities of both the 1st and 3rd Battalions, having already diverted the 2nd Battalion South Staffords from their original task in order to reinforce the drive for the Bridge, aware of Frost's growing plight, and suffering from a further succession of wireless failures, he now had news of another setback.

The second lift had been delayed.

It was difficult to understand why it had been held up by the weather, for the sky over Arnhem was bright and clear and only a slight breeze rustled the curtains in the HQ windows. In England, though, low cloud and fog drifted over the airfields. Out on the landing and dropping zones, Boy Wilson and his teams prepared their markers. Like everyone else, they had been led to understand that any aircraft which appeared would be ours; yet suddenly out of the pale sun twenty Me 109s dived, strafing the zones and setting fire to a number of the deserted gliders. The Independent Company leapt for cover.

By early afternoon, messages reaching Divisional HQ suggested that the South Staffords' efforts to get through were no more successful than those tried by others. They had run into tough opposition. Hicks therefore decided that they should now be supported not only by the remainder of their own battalion arriving with the second lift but also by Hackett's

11th Battalion. It was clearly going to upset Hackett's brigade plan – an advance to the north – but Hicks considered it was absolutely necessary.

When the second lift arrived, Charles Mackenzie and Gordon Grieve, one of my staff officers, drove off to break the news to Hackett. Following the railway line, they presently came upon scattered actions on both sides of the tracks. The Germans had made a bold bid to interfere with the safe arrival of the second lift on Groote Heide, an enormous expanse of heather and shrubland north of the Arnhem–Ede road. Earlier in the day, when the second lift had been scheduled to arrive, hardly a shot had been fired in the immediate area of the zone. This was largely due to the efforts of the KOSBs under a tough, ruddy complexioned lieutenant-colonel named Payton-Reid who had no respect whatever for Germans.

The KOSBs, who on landing the day before had formed up to the skirl of the pipes playing *Blue Bonnets*, had spent an exciting night and had then stopped a number of enemy armoured cars and other vehicles along the main road.

By mid-morning, the landing zone was firmly protected, but then the Germans became more active and Payton-Reid had to adopt a series of strong measures to fulfil his task of keeping the landing areas free from German interference. He suspected that there might be some German activity in a nearby wood and sent an officer and a sergeant-major to reconnoitre. Soon, there were sounds of firing which suggested the start of a sharp action. The sergeant-major came out in some alarm. 'The place is full of 'em, sir,' he reported. Payton-Reid was arranging to have the Germans dealt with when the officer, who was popularly called Glaxo, appeared from the pines, a rifle over his shoulder, and announced: 'A most excellent morning's shooting, Colonel. Two with my own gun.' Although the KOSBs generally had control, the Germans tested the defensive positions in the afternoon.

Ever since the first landing, Bittrich and his staff had expected our second lift. Communication had been established with one of the German fortresses in that part of the Channel area which had so far escaped the Allied advance. From this overrun but still operational pocket, the German High Command arranged for early warning of any further lifts. And three-quarters of an hour before the air columns of the second lift appeared over Arnhem, the Germans knew that they were on the way. A mobile reserve of SS, held back for just such a purpose, now headed for the likely landing area. At some points, the street fighting died down as units moved off. Anti-aircraft guns serving the ground battle were trailed off to positions from which they could contest the landings. For a brief spell, the German troops were encouraged by the appearance of the Luftwaffe as it struck around the landing areas. But as the sky began to fill with the gliders and parachutes and the throb of the seemingly endless chain of aircraft, there were men even among the SS units who, as a German officer was later to tell me, 'wilted with fear'.

In order to clear out some Germans who had got rather too close to part of the landing zones, and who could not be winkled out by fire, Payton-Reid led a bayonet charge. Some of the Germans fled, but there remained others in the fields and woods and ditches to shoot at the gliders and parachutists. An air burst ripped the fuselage of the Dakota carrying the second-in-command of the 11th Battalion, an athletic and gallant soldier called Dickie Lonsdale who was soon to leave his mark on this battle. Two parachutists were hit in the leg and prevented from jumping and Lonsdale had a badly gashed hand as he jumped. One aircraft with sixteen parachutists aboard was struck and set alight, but every man was able to leap clear. The American crew stayed and died with their aircraft. A glider, swerving off track, alighted belly-wise on the tops of the trees and remained there, torn, its jeep and anti-tank gun hanging grotesquely in the branches.

The heath was aflame in places now, giving an impression of a landing much less successful than in fact it was turning out to be: the wind which fanned the flames carried some parachutists off course into the woods.

As the force came over the dropping zone, Hackett, who was the first of his stick, noticed when the light went on that they were still about 1000 yards from the exact jumping point. He stood in the door, admiring the view and feeling elated because he so easily recognized the topographical features on which he had based his rendezvous arrangements. He could see the coloured smoke indicating the rallying point; the intersection of ditch and copse and, beyond on the main road, the restaurant. All this he took in during the extra seconds he was allowing himself – one, two, three, four, five. Then he was away.

As his parachute opened, the sudden tug caused him to drop his walking-stick. There was some shooting, and he saw other parachutists floating down. On the ground, he was pleased to see that he had touched down less than 300 yards from the spot chosen as his Brigade HQ. He began to root round the heather for his stick. I dare say that if I had been present I would have made some appropriate remark about this concern of his for walking-sticks. Some time earlier, when I had visited his brigade in Rutland, he had taxed me about the rightful ownership of my walking-stick. 'It's remarkably like one I lost when I was last at Divisional headquarters,' he said.

I assured him that the stick was mine.

'I bought mine in Oakham, where I live,' he persisted, 'and it was an ashplant stick exactly like this one.'

I indicated the 'U' which was carved in the stick I was carrying. 'There,' I said. 'That leaves no room for doubt.'

Despite this, Hacket plainly suspected that I had purloined his stick and that the 'U' was merely a criminal attempt to cover my misdeed. He was annoyed, and I thought he was merely being silly.

The one he had just dropped as he came down was a replacement bought in London and he was concerned not to lose it. In the midst of the battle developing around him, he searched the heather. He came across a parachutist who was in severe pain with a stomach wound sustained on the way down, and arranged for him to be attended. Then he found, cowering in the heather, no fewer than ten frightened Germans who showed that they wished to surrender.

'Wait here,' Hackett ordered severely in German, one of the languages he had learned to speak well. 'I'll see to you presently.' He continued the search for his stick, miraculously stumbled on it and then returned to collect his prisoners and march them to his HQ.

Soon afterwards, the staff officers from Divisional HQ, Mackenzie and Grieve, appeared through a long narrow culvert under the railway, having already encountered Lieutenant-Colonel George Lea and some of the 11th Battalion. Mackenzie realized that the news he brought would not please Hackett, and wished that I had also informed the Brigadiers of my chain of command decision. As quickly as he could, Mackenzie explained that I had disappeared and that Hicks was now in command of the division.

Hackett registered a mild protest, and was reluctant to accept that I had placed Hicks before him.

'Well, there it is,' Mackenzie said placatingly. 'You will only upset the works if you try to do anything about it.'

The 4th Parachute Brigade was moving off to a good start despite the German interference. As the little group of officers watched them, Mackenzie added: 'The plan now is for 11th Battalion to move in support of the drive for the Bridge, immediately.'

Sharply reacting to this, Hackett said that it cut across his notions as a commander to be told how to dispose the troops under his command, instead of being given a task to do. 'I don't like to be told that one of my battalions has already been nominated,' he added. 'As it happens, it is the right one to send.' Hackett, with his own task in mind, asked if he might take the KOSB battalion, which was still defending the landing area, under his command in lieu of the 11th Battalion. This was presently agreed.

Mackenzie was troubled as he drove back with the certain feeling that Hackett was unhappy about the new arrangement. The commander of the 4th Parachute Brigade had been quick to see that the 11th Battalion was the obvious one to send into town because it was so much nearer the objective, having come down on the south-eastern corner of the zone, whereas the 10th Battalion was farther north and the 156th Battalion to the west. Nevertheless, Mackenzie felt anxious.

During the afternoon, Divisional HQ had moved to the

Hartenstein Hotel, and Mackenzie had hardly got back when he was summoned to the telephone. It was a Dutch naval officer, Lieutenant-Commander Wolters, who had joined the division some days before the operation as a liaison with the Dutch people and Resistance groups. A brave and capable officer who was to be of great help to the division, Wolters had gone into Arnhem right at the start and returned with information about the German set-up, and had also arranged for the Dutch telephone exchange in Arnhem to supply us with information. What he had to say now, in a tone which suggested his information was correct, gave Mackenzie a jolt. 'There are sixty tanks coming down the road into Arnhem from the north,' Wolters said.

'Which road?' Mackenzie asked.

'They are on the main road north of Deelen airfield.'

Mackenzie now recalled those vague and unconfirmed stories about the re-fitting panzer corps about which he had been given so little information by 2nd Army. Nevertheless, he was slightly incredulous. 'Are you sure about this?' he asked. 'I think you'd better get the information checked.'

Wolters went off the line and an hour or so later he telephoned again to confirm the report.

It gave Mackenzie a sinking feeling.

As the evening wore on, the division was scattered and the drive to support Frost halted. The 11th Battalion, and two companies of South Staffords with whom they had marched out from the dropping zone, had entered the western fringe of Arnhem and were not far from the place where I was trapped with Taylor and Cleminson. Other South Staffords – those previously diverted by Hicks – were held up in the houses, as were the 1st and 3rd Battalions. At Divisional HQ a South Staffords officer reported that his battalion was out of touch with the 1st and 3rd Battalions, though there had in fact been a link-up in the vicinity of the St Elizabeth Hospital after a dusk clash with the Germans. Other rumours were wafting around the division. It was said that I had reached Frost at the Bridge and also that I was a prisoner. In fact, I was still in a mood of reluctant contemplation lying on a bed in the small front upstairs room at 14 Zwarteweg around midnight, when Hackett turned up at Divisional HQ to clear up what he described as 'a grossly untidy situation'.

Since his meeting with Mackenzie, Hackett had rationalized Hicks's succession to command as having been contingent on his own absence from the division. He did not want to stand on any ceremony about it, but the point might arise; for Hacket was disturbed not only by the command development but also by the task given to his 11th Battalion. By the time he reached the Hartenstein Hotel, having driven down from Wolfhezen, he was angry. The sky was lit by the fireworks of battle; but things were reasonably quiet in the divisional area. The ground-floor dining-room of the hotel was laid out with tables and maps, and all the paper paraphernalia of staff work, and Hackett was reminded of manoeuvres back in England.

In a corner of this room, the two brigadiers, between whom there never had existed a great deal of sympathy, met to thrash out the problems that were exercising Hackett. Hicks, the professional infantryman, tall, amiably reserved and practical; Hackett, small, volatile, an ex-armoured regiment commander – I had once, in a joking moment, called him 'that broken-down cavalryman' – and with a keen brain formidable in its range. Hackett led off by asking what orders had been given to the 11th Battalion, and was told that the Battalion had been given a route, a warning that another battalion would be operating in the vicinity, and orders to do what it could to help the 1st Parachute Brigade. Visualizing the possibilities of a mix-up, he asked who was in overall command. Hicks explained that the battalions were working individually.

'It is clearly unsatisfactory from the point of view of a normal command set-up,' Hicks said. Normally the two units would have been under Lathbury's command but as he was missing and his HQ, or the effective part of it, was at the Bridge, this was out of the question. In Hicks's mind was the plight of Frost at the Bridge, and somewhat pointedly he emphasized that it would be ridiculous not to help the 2nd Battalion in whatever way they could.

Hackett agreed, but he wanted a tidier plan.

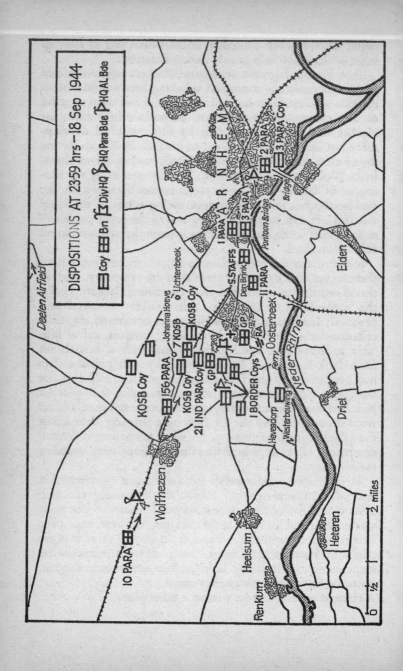

The role assigned to Hackett's 4th Brigade the following morning, a move into Arnhem from the north-west, also caused some hard words. 'I must have an objective,' Hackett said, 'and I think we should first take the high ground east of Johanna Hoeve. I will then see what I can undertake to assist the operations in Arnhem, and I want a series of times so that I can relate my action to anyone else's.'

Unless a plan on those lines was made, said Hackett, he would be compelled to raise the question of command of the division. My senior administrative officer, Henry Preston, entered the room and Hicks, turning to him, said: 'Brigadier Hackett thinks he ought to be in command of the division.' As Hackett started to disclaim any such ambition, Preston went outside and told the duty officer to rouse Mackenzie. He did so with the words: 'Come down quickly. The two Brigadiers are having a flaming row!'

When Mackenzie appeared the worst was over, and the brigadiers had agreed on a plan which involved Hackett's Brigade taking the high ground at Koepel.

I know now that I should have told all three brigadiers, as well as Mackenzie, of my chain of command decision. I had not made it lightly. Lathbury was the senior brigadier, and Hicks, by seniority in his rank, the junior; Hicks was the oldest by several years, and Hackett by a long way the youngest. Hicks and Lathbury were both infantrymen, Hackett a cavalryman. I was satisfied that Lathbury should be my immediate successor, but I was less sure about the sequence after that. Although Hackett was next in seniority, my opinion in those days of brigadiers of cavalry was not of the highest, due to earlier experience, and I considered that Hicks was more experienced in the handling of battalions on the ground. Therefore, I told Mackenzie that in the event of Lathbury also becoming a casualty, then Hicks was to take over.

I considered, rightly or wrongly, that the mere fact of knowing that I had given precedence to Hicks would prove unsettling to Hackett and might even seem to be a reflection on his ability as a commander, which I had no intention of suggesting. Hackett was so much younger and had not the experience which later made him a most successful commander of an armoured division in Germany. In restricting my order to Mackenzie, I regarded the succession after Lathbury as being hardly more than academic. I had no intention of becoming a casualty, and the prospect of Lathbury also being put out represented a fairly long shade of odds.

On the upper floor of 14 Zwarteweg, Taylor, Cleminson and I waited for signs of the British attack we were expecting. There had been nothing to suggest that the second lift might have been seriously delayed by the weather, and I wondered if they had made a good start. From time to time during the night we got up to stretch ourselves and also to glance into the street where the self-propelled gun was still stationed. We took it in turns to keep watch and although I kept reminding myself that a commander in battle must never neglect his sleep, my mind was too active for sound rest. How far had XXX Corps advanced? Had the Americans succeeded at Grave and Nijmegen? Perhaps by now the 2nd Battalion had been given some help? I wondered if Heaps and his roving companions with the Bren carriers had managed to get through with supplies to the Bridge? It was very restricting in the little house and my frustration was increasing. I must have slept for a short time, then I awoke with a dull pain across my chest. I felt for the sore spot. My fingers touched one of the two hand grenades inside my smock. I had been lying on them and the pressure had bruised me slightly. At that moment, we heard the wheeze of the engine of the self-propelled gun outside followed by shouts and the rattle of its tracks. It was moving off. And now the middle-aged Dutchman appeared and announced excitedly that the British were at the bottom of the road.

We were in such a hurry to join them that we left a Sten gun on the shelf, and the family kept it for some time as a souvenir. We ran down the street, and I thanked God we had made contact again. The men were South Staffords with several 11th Battalion parachutists. An officer of the South Staffords told me something of the situation and said that this party had been sent by Hicks to help the drive into the town. 'Your HQ is now at the Hartenstein Hotel in Ooster-beek,' he added. Although heartened by the evidence that the second lift was with us, albeit after a delay, I could see that some confusion existed – locally at least. It was imperative that I should get back to my HQ as quickly as possible and take a grip on the battle. I was unaware that at this precise moment, Lea, commanding the 11th Battalion, and Derek McCardie, commanding the South Staffords, were only about a hundred yards away trying to co-ordinate a push into the town. As it turned out, it would have been better if I had stayed a little longer to assess the local situation thereabouts and to co-ordinate these thrusts personally; for in the desperate and confused hours before us it became only too painfully clear that what was needed above all else was some co-ordination among the units fighting their way into Arnhem. If I had known this, I would have taken control on the spot. Instead, I borrowed a jeep and started to drive very fast for my HQ at Oosterbeek. Taylor came with me, but Cleminson preferred to try to rejoin the 3rd Battalion. 'They must be around here somewhere,' he said hopefully. 'I'll catch up with them.'

Once again, I took the lower road which included that steep stretch exposed to the snipers across the river. I advised Taylor to duck and hold tight. I put my foot down hard. Sure enough, the bullets pinged around us so that not for the first time, and certainly not the last, I felt like an Aunt Sally on a shooting range. We were untouched, however, and the jeep held the corner at the bottom quite well.

# CHAPTER FOUR

As Taylor and I reached the Arnhem–Utrecht road, we heard the German mortaring. Unsure as to the exact location of the Hartenstein, we stopped to inquire of a group of soldiers. They were tired and looked as if they had been in a fight, and I was reminded of my own unkempt appearance. Soon we reached the hotel, an unmistakable white building which today has the appearance of a restful roadhouse. As yet, it had hardly been touched by the battle, though there were a few slit trenches and the lawns were laid out with markers for pilots who were due to fly supplies to us during the day. The windows were still intact and a curtain flapped in the faint morning breeze. In the woods round the hotel there was a lot of movement; there were jeeps under the spreading trees and an anti-tank gun with its sharp end facing challengingly towards Arnhem. Every now and again, a mortar bomb exploded.

It was 7.25 am.

Mackenzie greeted me with as much warmth as anyone could be expected to muster in such conditions. 'We had assumed, sir,' he said meaningfully, 'that you had gone for good.'

He explained how the command had reverted to Hicks, who was now looking round his own brigade, and described the modifications already made to the original plan. It was a disturbing picture and what stood out a mile was the need to infuse some overall direction into the separate moves to join Frost. As Hicks was expected back within a few minutes, I decided to await his return. The diminutive and always cheerful figure of Hancock now appeared in the hallway. 'I'm glad you're back, sir,' he observed. 'Your tea and shaving water are ready.' In the most unsettled situations in desert or built-up area Hancock had never failed to produce a mug of tea, and enough water for a shave, and there had been times in the Middle East when his facility for producing water in the most arid conditions had caused me to ponder his natural talents as a diviner.

I felt better already.

Hicks was not long in arriving. He was worried about the activities in the town, for he had had no news of the 1st and 3rd Battalions. It was now that I realized how much better it would have been for me to have stopped in the St Elizabeth Hospital area for a little time in order to tie up the advance of the 1st and 3rd, the 11th Battalion and the South Staffords.

It was nearly 8 am.

'Someone will have to get down into the town right away to co-ordinate these attacks,' I said. 'It will have to be a senior officer.'

We summoned Hilary Barlow, Hicks's second-in-command of the Airlanding Brigade, who was just the man to take on such an assignment. He set off with a wireless set in the back of his jeep, and was never seen again. There were unconfirmed reports that his jeep had been noticed about half way between the Hartenstein Hotel and St Elizabeth Hospital. I believe that Barlow may have been trapped on that exposed riverside stretch. The fact remains that he was one of the few among the officers and men who died at Arnhem of whom no trace was ever found.

Having examined the divisional situation, I was not convinced that Hackett should continue trying for the high ground to the north. The air plan would also have to be altered, for it seemed that the Poles who were due to arrive in the third lift were in for a sticky reception. I ordered a signal to be sent requesting that the Poles' dropping zone should be changed and warning 38 and 36 Groups of the RAF that our supply dropping point north of Warnsborn was now well outside the area held by the division. These messages, however, did not get through.

During the morning, such scant information as we got was far from encouraging. Enemy concentrations in the woods north of landing zone B; the South Staffords and elements of the 11th Battalion in trouble on the main road about a mile from the bridge; more enemy tanks arriving in Arnhem from Apeldoorn. Further, we now received news that the leading tanks of XXX Corps had only reached Grave. It meant that Horrocks was already some thirty hours behind schedule. Despite our uncertain communications, and the shortage of information which this involved, it was possible to visualize XXX Corps being held up for some time on the single highway that stretched northwards towards us.

Actually, at this stage of the morning the spearheads of the Guards Armoured Division, having crossed the sappers' new bridge at Zon, had advanced through the corridor to the woodland south of Nijmegen where they found Jim Gavin's 82nd Airborne Division engaged in beating off furious German counter-attacks from the Reichswald Forest. The Americans were losing some of the finest airborne soldiers the world has known. It was close and bloody fighting. No attack could be made on the Nijmegen bridge until the afternoon, and when it was launched the Germans were firmly placed in the fortified defences of Huner Park. Tanks were knocked out. Parachutists and Guards were pinned as they tried to infiltrate towards the bridge. The bridge was still very firmly in German hands.

At this time we had news from our Bridge at Arnhem, where Frost's force was fighting among the houses at the northern end. It looked as though Hackett would have to be diverted from his northern thrust. During the morning, Mackenzie and Loder-Symonds had visited him, and I set off to see him along the route they had taken. The KOSBs, under Payton-Reid, had gone during the night for the high ground at Koepel only to be seen off by machine-guns and, to avoid being caught in the open in daylight, Payton-Reid had wisely pulled back to positions along the roadside close to Johanna Hoeve Farm. Another battalion under Hackett, the 156th, was preparing a further assault on Lichtenbeek, with the 10th Parachute Battalion on its left directed on to a road junction.

Our operations map showed the increasing German build-up which included tank formations. Unless I acted quickly, there was every possibility that the division would be defeated in detail. I took the road leading north-east from the hotel towards the railway junction at Halt Oosterbeek. I came upon a group of Recce Squadron soldiers who had been driven over the crossing near Lichtenbeek, and I then made a detour towards the main road, cutting through a built-up area which led me to the railway side. There were all the signs of a real battle brewing towards Wolfhezen, and it was apparent that unless I was going to chance my luck in that direction, either at Wolfhezen crossing, or at the culvert under the tracks, I would have to leave my jeep on the south side and climb over the embankment and across the railway. I checked with the map, and decided that this was the better approach. I walked a short distance along the railway and then came on Hackett and his HQ on the edge of a thickly wooded copse at the far side. A rutted track ran right through their positions. As I slithered down the grassy bank to meet him, I saw Hackett glance sharply upwards and then heard approaching fighters and the chatter of machine-guns. The Luftwaffe again! Only three Me 109s this time, but they forced us to dive to the ground as they strafed the area with guns and small bombs. 'I'm delighted to see you're out of it, sir,' Hackett said. 'There were all sorts of ugly rumours. As you can see, we're pinned down right along the line.' He indicated a distinctive tree-covered ridge to the east which was busy with small-arms and mortar fire; a fierce local engagement by the looks of it. 'The Boche are shooting from the woods to the north and beyond to the east.' Already, he had tried several times to get on. And now, as a result of Loder-Symonds's visit earlier, he was receiving fire support from one of the light batteries sited deep in Oosterbeek. It was all making little impression on the Germans.

Looking through my field glasses, I could see a few hundred yards away the rear elements of the two battalions which were stretched in a long thin line. With all his men committed, Hackett could not contemplate an outflanking movement. 'Unless the enemy alters his plans in such a way as to favour us,' he told me, 'there's not much future for the brigade in its present line of advance.' He still had a long way to go along this defended axis of the railway to the Arnhem–Amsterdam road in order to take up his sector of the original bridgehead. It all added up to a confirmation of the thoughts with which I had set out; yet the strength of the opposition already encountered in the town by the 1st and 3rd Battalions and those who had gone to their assistance suggested that it might still be wrong to precipitate the 4th Brigade into a drastic switch. It might be that Hackett would be able to make progress eventually along his present line, or even farther north. What was more important was to tie up his actions with those of the rest of the division. I discussed with him a plan to withdraw the 4th Brigade south across the railway with a fresh line of advance along the Arnhem–Heelsum road – the middle road. But I urged him not to pursue this plan immediately. I wanted first to re-examine the complete divisional position.

I set off back for the hotel.

Hardly half an hour after my departure, Hackett learned that the Border Regiment had been taken on to the south of him by a force of Germans near the river in the Renkum–Heelsum region. Unless he was quick about seizing and holding the Wolfhezen crossing – his only exit for vehicles and anti-tank guns south of the highly-banked railway track – there was a risk that the Germans might get between 4th Brigade and Hicks's Airlanding Brigade. The situation was so fraught with awful possibilities that Hackett promptly ordered the 10th Battalion to disengage and to withdraw west to the crossing which was to be held in readiness for the southward move of the entire brigade. It had to be done quickly, otherwise he might be caught without a crossing.

Back at Divisional HQ, I weighed the information seeping through from the Airlanding Brigade guarding our back door and from the units fighting their way into the town. I contacted Hackett and ordered him to disengage and to move towards Arnhem on an axis south of the railway.

Our northern arc was done.

And now, in this fateful afternoon of Tuesday, September 19th, everything began to go awry. The Airlanding Brigade, to the west and north-west, was under severe attack; there were all the distant signs that Hackett was in some difficulty to the north, and in the town casualties mounted among the units making separate bids to break through. From every side we could hear the sounds of battle. The imagination of some of the troops not yet engaged was working overtime.

Rumours spread – wild, fantastic rumours with no basis in fact. There were small parties of hurrying soldiers, obviously uncontrolled, and then twenty or more, under a young officer, dashed across the lawn in front of the Hartenstein shouting, 'The Germans are coming!' With Mackenzie, I moved to intercept them. They were young soldiers whose self-control had momentarily deserted them. I shouted at them, and I had to intervene physically. It is unpleasant to have to restrain soldiers by force and threats, as now we had to do. We ordered them back into the positions they had deserted, and I had a special word with the tall young officer who in his panic had set such a disgraceful example. I could read their inward feelings by the expressions in their eyes. I am sure that the willpower and courage required in battle are very different to the quality commonly called 'guts' when it is related to such sports as horse-riding and boxing. Contact with the enemy means that men are up against not so much an obvious, visual problem as the unknown, the unexpected and the unsuspected. It is their willpower or character which counts and, as Lord Moran once wrote, the main essential is to have control of one's willpower and that is a question of conscience, which comes back to character.

In the desert and other theatres of war attempts were generally made to blood new divisions slowly by giving them initially a quiet area to look after and by the attachment of key men to formations which knew the form. There is no opportunity to attune airborne soldiers gradually. They are in it up to the neck right away. I had no doubt that many of these jittery men who now faced us would behave quite differently once they had settled down and would turn out to be as resolute as the best. It was, however, interesting to note that they came from certain units which were weaker than others as regards their state of training, morale and leadership. Nevertheless, it was distressing to see this flash of panic which could have been contagious. There were other signs of the early unease and edginess – indiscriminate shooting, unnecessary visits by soldiers to the Hartenstein cellars. Mackenzie, going round the HQ defences, came upon a slit trench, now deserted and containing a loaded Bren and a nest of grenades.

I impressed on commanders the need to stop this wild, haphazard shooting. Apart from the fact that it was unsettling, it was an arrant waste of ammunition, which we could not afford.

There were even more setbacks to come this day. Our signals requesting changed dropping points for supplies were not received, so now we were forced to witness the first act of the re-supply tragedy of Arnhem as the RAF crews flew through violent and intense flak in order to drop their loads accurately – on dropping points which we no longer held. On the ground, the troops tried by every means possible to attract the attention of these gallant crews: they waved, they paid out parachute material, they lit beacons. Into the deadly anti-aircraft fire the aircraft came on at a thousand feet maintaining courses without a single exception until their loads were delivered. Only to us on the ground was the agonizing irony of all this known. The Germans were getting most of the stuff. One Dakota was hit by flak and the starboard wing set on fire. Yet it came on, descending to 900 feet. It seemed that every anti-aircraft gun in the vicinity was sighted on the crippled aircraft. With its starboard engine blazing, it came through to the dropping zone. At the end of the run, the Dakota turned and made a second run to drop the remaining supplies. From foxholes and slit trenches and from the restricted spaces to which we were trying to attract the pilots; from blasted buildings and ditches and emplacements of rubble and earth, the eyes of hundreds and probably thousands of careworn soldiers gazed upwards through the battle haze. We were spellbound and speechless, and I daresay there is not a survivor of Arnhem who will ever forget, or want to forget, the courage we were privileged to witness in those terrible eight minutes. It was not until some time after the operation that I learned the name of the pilot of that Dakota – Flight-Lieutenant David Lord, of 271 Squadron. We saw the machine crashing in flames as one of its wings collapsed, and we did not know that Lord had ordered his crew to abandon while making no effort to leave himself. There was one survivor.

This incident was talked about long afterwards by men who

had grown accustomed to bravery, and in November, 1945, Flight-Lieutenant Lord, DFC, was awarded a posthumous Victoria Cross. Of 163 aircraft which attempted to bring us supplies that afternoon, thirteen were lost and ninety-seven others were damaged by flak. And despite our signals – yellow smoke, yellow triangles, scarf waving, and the rest – the best part of 390 tons of food and ammunition fell to the Germans. A few canisters which fell off target, and there were only a few, were picked up by the collectors from Michael Packe's RASC units.

The events of this black afternoon were not yet over. In withdrawing to take the Wolfhezen crossing, the 10th Battalion found that their rendezvous was under fire, and in the fighting that ensued their casualties were high. Hardly had they emerged from this and continued their move when the Poles began to arrive on a glider landing zone which lay between the 10th Battalion and the enemy. The Germans, well-placed to receive the Poles, opened up with flak, tracer, mortars and machine-guns – and the hapless 10th Battalion, already pressed from behind by Germans determined to make their withdrawal a costly one, were now faced with fire from the Poles who mistook them for the enemy. In the confusion, which was not eased by the different gear worn by the Poles and their grey berets, identities were not established until some lives had been lost. As Hackett was later to put it, the situation required 'great energy by the officers of the brigade headquarters to prevent more confusion'.

To the unfortunate Poles it must have seemed that no friends existed at all. Payton-Reid had sent a KOSB company to help the Poles unload their gliders, but again at first it was a case of mistaken identity and the Poles opened fire. Meanwhile Payton-Reid had been summoned from his battalion by Hackett who now gave him the withdrawal plan. It was surprising to Payton-Reid, for he had left a quiet area. 'We are not even in contact,' he said. Even so, he had to come out and keep the railway culvert open for brigade traffic. When he returned to his own battalion area, he found there had just been a sharp engagement. His second-in-command, a major named Coke, oozed assurance as he reported: 'We've just had a hell of a battle. The Boche attacked, and we've seen him off. Sergeant Graham must have killed fifty himself with a Vickers and Drum-Major Tate had a real bang with a Bren.' Silence reigned now and Payton-Reid was prompted to ask, 'Well, what's happened to them?'

'Gone,' Coke replied. 'They've cleared off.'

After this successful skirmish, it seemed odd to be ordered to withdraw – 'and damned quick,' as Payton-Reid put it. The KOSBs were brimming with confidence. Yet two hours later they had lost nearly all their transport, two companies had been cut off, and reorganization was proving difficult. 'You just can't get up and rush away from the enemy in daylight like that,' one experienced soldier said angrily. 'You just can't bloody well do it.' Elsewhere, the Germans were making the withdrawal of the rest of Hackett's Brigade a costly business. Neither the 10th nor the 156th Battalions were given any pause by their SS pursuers. The 10th especially was given a pounding, but the parachutists' resistance was such as to cause the Germans facing them one of the highest casualty rates among all the German units employed in the battle.

An officer of the 10th Battalion, Captain L. E. Queripel, persistently crossed a road which was under enemy fire to position his men. He picked up a wounded NCO and carried him to cover, and was hit in the face. Then he moved on a German strongpoint consisting of two machine-guns and a captured British anti-tank gun which had been causing casualties among his men, and killed the crew of three. The gun was recaptured. As the Germans closely harassed the withdrawing troops, Queripel and a party of men took up a covering position in a ditch. He was wounded in the face and both arms, and the party were short of weapons and ammunition, though they had a few Mills bombs, rifles and pistols. And as the SS Grenadiers closed in, hurtling stick bombs into the ditch, Queripel promptly hurled them back. Soon, most of those who had shared his last stand were dead or badly wounded, and Queripel ordered the survivors to get clear while he covered their exit with a final bout of grenade throwing. He was last seen alone and still fighting in the ditch.

Queripel won a posthumous Victoria Cross.

As the survivors of the 10th Battalion came out of this pounding towards the crossing, Hackett marvelled at their discipline and spirit. They came over the railway some 250 strong. By now, the 156th Battalion had only some 270 officers and men.

It had been an expensive afternoon.

To make this worse, some of the now precious transport was bogged down in the sandy ground north of the tracks. And the Germans already had the range and began to shell the new positions, while the rattle and whine of their tanks and self-propelled guns could be distinctly heard.

Meanwhile, in the town the mixed force – the remnants of the 1st and 3rd Battalions of the 1st Parachute Brigade, the South Staffords and the 11th Battalion – was in even worse shape. Throughout the day since I had left the St Elizabeth Hospital area, the attrition had proceeded in the streets of western Arnhem. The South Staffords had pushed through to capture a building called the Monastery, while to the right nearer the river those who were left of the 1st and 3rd Battalions were having a very rough time as tanks and self-propelled guns got among them. Lacking anti-tank guns which could not be brought up because of the Germans' grip on the main road, some parachutists were using their Piats with deadly effect and economy and in some instances mortars were being fired almost vertically. The advanced elements of two companies of the 1st Battalion got to within half a mile of the Bridge and there were reports of bayonet charges and that one company was down to eight men and another to six.

This little party had fought itself closer to John Frost and the Bridge garrison than anyone was to reach during the rest of the battle. They left behind them many wounded in the houses bordering their route.

When Jimmy Cleminson linked up with his Battalion after leaving me, he was dismayed to see that it had been so reduced. The men were in action close by the Pavilion, where Cleminson came on a 3rd Battalion officer, Richard Dorrien-Smith, and two officers of the 1st Battalion.

The scene was now one of disorderly retreat as stragglers came back in the direction of Oosterbeek. 'We'll have to

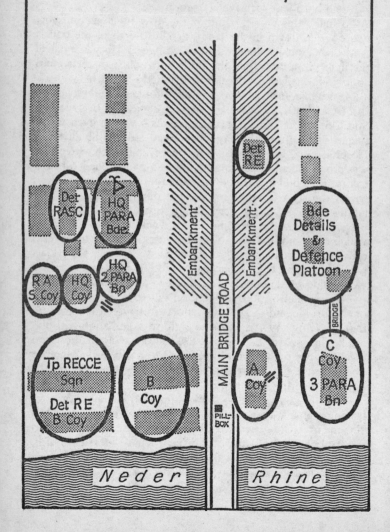

Approximate positions
2 PARA Bn & ATTACHED TROOPS
ARNHEM BRIDGE — 17–21 Sep. 1944

pull out if this goes on,' said Dorrien-Smith. 'You'd better find somewhere for us to reorganize with the men we have left.' Cleminson went as fast as he could along a road littered with the debris of battle, and he overtook many battle-wearied men going in the same direction.

Not far away from the scene of the 3rd Battalion's action the South Staffords, after attacking a tank with Brens set up on the roadside, were driven into a dell on the town side of the Monastery. Their Piat ammunition was finished. In comparative safety the German tanks now rattled up into the dell and shot into it. There were many casualties. Another company of the South Staffords tried to take the high ground at Den Brink which had earlier proved such an obstacle. They were driven off.

In the bitter, confused fighting on the western outskirts of Arnhem, there was by this time chaos. Nobody knew what was happening; more and more troops took the road back to Oosterbeek in front of the German armour. They were jaded and disorganized and many were carrying on despite their wounds. Sheriff Thompson, the lieutenant-colonel commanding the 1st Light Regiment whose batteries had been very busy since they landed, especially in support of Frost and Hackett, left his command post at Oosterbeek to drive along the twisting road in the direction of Arnhem in order to assess how his three batteries might help the thrusts into the town with fire support.

He came upon straggling parties of men moving despondently and in disorder towards Oosterbeek. He realized that this would not do, and that they must be collected. He tried to get them into position on the line of the railway just west of Den Brink. Presently, there were the remnants of the 1st, 3rd and 11th Battalions and the South Staffords. All had lost their commanders. Sheriff Thompson later reported to me what he had done, and I was indebted to him for the lucid picture he was able to present of what was going on in the town as well as for the reorganization. Dickie Lonsdale, second-in-command of the 11th Battalion and the most senior officer with the mixed force, was ordered to take command of it.

The railway line along which Thompson had attempted to get the mixed force into position continued northwards across the main Arnhem–Oosterbeek road, and it was on this line, astride the road, that I intended Hackett and his 4th Brigade should stop to reorganize before they went for the Bridge.

With the re-formation in progress and Hackett continuing to extricate his brigade from the north I summoned Graeme Warrack, our chief doctor, a substantial and prematurely bald thirty-one years old colonel with an air about him of great physical strength and conviviality. His Red Cross jeeps had been busily scouring the area. 'Let's go and see some of the chaps in the dressing stations,' I said.

He seemed delighted. We set out on foot just as another mortar 'hate' was working up. Casualties had been mounting fast, and the hotel which was being used as a dressing station now had several annexes among the neighbouring houses. Even so, the place was choc-a-bloc with wounded, some too badly hurt for conversation, others eager for encouraging news as I approached. I stopped by one man with a reddening head bandage and an arm in a sling. I asked him where he had run into trouble. 'In the town,' he said ruefully. 'One of those bloody SPs, sir. How's the 2nd Army getting on?'

Everyone in the ward who was conscious knew as well as I did that we were almost beyond the accepted time limit for an airborne division to survive without reinforcement. Standing so that all could hear, I said: 'We haven't much in the way of news, but I'm sure it's only a question of a very short time before we link up.' Walking among these wounded men, I sensed their irritation at having been put out of the battle so early. As I left, they were wishing *me* good luck and the orderlies were removing a corpse.

Warrack and his officers and men seemed to have the medical situation well in hand. Earlier, shortly after I had got back to Divisional HQ, I had suggested to Warrack that he ought to find out what was going on at the St Elizabeth Hospital where I had personally seen so much activity, and that he might use the Dutch public telephone service. Calling from a doctor's house near his own HQ, he got through easily and soon found himself talking to a medical officer,

Derek Ridler, who could hardly get over his surprise at being called to a phone booth in the middle of a battle. Although some medical officers had been removed from the hospital by the Germans, the rest were coping adequately with eighty wounded officers and men. The discussion was punctuated by explosions and small-arms fire. 'There's a fair battle going on outside,' Ridler explained. He also told Warrack that Lathbury had been in the hospital for attention.

As dusk approached to herald our third night north of the Neder Rhine, the enemy laid on the heaviest mortaring so far. I met a number of Resistance men who were making determined and daring journeys in order to feed us with information, especially about the disposition of tanks and other armour. It had built up heavily, particularly between us and the Bridge. There was no news of the progress of XXX Corps, and as yet no indication that our Tactical Air Force had done much to slow the German build-up around us.

Reports showed that both Hackett and Lonsdale were under pressure. In fact, near the river, the German tanks tried to cut through the positions which Lonsdale had now taken up. Three of them emerged from a wood and Sergeant Baskerfield of the South Staffords, at a crossroads with his anti-tank gun, knocked out the leading tank with his first shot and disabled the second. Under cover of the third tank German infantry tried to cross the road but were stopped. Baskerfield's gun was knocked out and he took over another whose crew had been killed. He fought the third tank alone until he was shot through the head.

He won a posthumous Victoria Cross.

The survivors of the 3rd Battalion who were in action near the railway were now ordered by Lonsdale to pull back and join the remainder of the mixed force near the Oosterbeek Church. Dorrien-Smith was killed as they retired, leaving Cleminson as the sole remaining officer. It was raining, and getting dark, and hushed but urgent voices summoned men into the church – a neat, square edifice, buttressed and with a belltower, and set well back off the road at the edge of the open polder alongside the river. Into the church came a lot of very tired and dirty soldiers, some of whom had been through a lot. They entered the tiny church, their boots echoing on the stone floor, and slumped in the pews while outside the din of battle grew ever more intense and the voices of officers and men guiding others to the church could be heard occasionally above the whine and crunch of the mortars.

Lonsdale now appeared, his hands in bandages. He looked down at the strained and desperate faces as he climbed the steps to the pulpit. In the congregation were survivors from the 1st, 3rd and 11th Battalions, the South Staffords and some glider pilots. Cleminson counted thirty-six men of his own battalion. Suddenly the place was hushed as Lonsdale, his hands gripping the edge of the pulpit, began: 'You know as well as I do there are a lot of bloody Germans coming at us. Well, all we can do is to stay here and hang on in the hope that somebody catches us up. We must fight for our lives and stick together.' From the distance came the rumble of heavy guns and outside the shattered windows the sky was lit with the pyrotechnics of battle. Above Lonsdale and beyond the damaged organ loft some rafters hung loose. The troops, several hundred in all, listened attentively, their blackened faces upturned. 'We've fought the Germans before – in North Africa, Sicily, Italy. They weren't good enough for us then, and they're bloody well not good enough for us now. They're up against the finest soldiers in the world. An hour from now you will take up defensive positions north of the road outside. Make certain you dig in well and that your weapons and ammo are in good order. We are getting short of ammo, so when you shoot you shoot to kill. Good luck to you all.'

And now they filed out, having wrung out their trousers and smocks and shirts. They were collected by units and organized for the defence. The South Staffords dug in near the church, with the remnants of the 1st and 3rd Battalions covering the open ground on the northern side of the lower Arnhem–Oosterbeek road, and the 11th Battalion on the road. The glider pilots under Major Robert Cain of the South Staffords had their own area beyond the 1st and 3rd Battalions' positions.

I had been out looking round the divisional area and when I returned to the hotel, Boy Wilson was waiting to report. Characteristically, he oozed optimism: this grandfather of paratroopers positively glowed in battle. 'They've been trying to tell us all the time you were a prisoner, sir,' he said cheerfully. 'We told 'em we didn't believe it.'

'You haven't been *talking* to these people, have you?'

'That's just it,' he said. 'We have.'

The Germans had brought up a loudspeaker through which they had blared the somewhat garbled information that I was a prisoner and that what was left of the division was now surrounded. 'It is better you should give yourselves up, Tommies.' Wilson's men answered with a Bren burst. They had enjoyed little respite since the initial landings, though the way Wilson described it they were finding life anything but uncongenial. 'They are terrified of the red berets,' Wilson exulted. 'They don't like us one bit.' At some stage, the Germans called on the Independent Company to surrender, and Wilson ordered one of his German-speaking troops to reply broadly on the lines that the company was too scared to venture out and that the Germans should send a party to fetch them. Wilson ordered his men to stand by. Nonetheless he was surprised when about fifty Germans emerged from the wood across the open field. Twelve Brens opened up simultaneously, and not a German escaped.

It had been quite a day at the Bridge. During Monday night, the battle had become sufficiently subdued for Frost and his men to pick up some sleep. Frost himself had slept only half an hour since leaving England. Before dawn he learned that there were still no signs of impending relief and in order to conserve ammunition for the attacks which he knew must come, he ordered that sniping should cease. Essential as it was, this order meant that the encroaching Germans were able further to improve their positions. Whenever one of the parachutists ventured out, the streets and spaces between the houses were sprayed with machine-gun fire. Movement became impossible in this lethal district. From the far bank of the river and also from the other side of the Bridge approach on the north side the Germans were blazing away with Spandaus.

About the only consolation Frost's force had during the day was the accurate and effective shooting controlled by Mumford of Sheriff Thompson's gunners who from Ooster-beek was dropping shells to the immense discomfort of the Panzergrenadiers besieging Frost. For some time the Germans had been using a number of 20-mm and 40-mm flak guns to cope with Frost's machine-guns; they now turned them on the church steeples in the town, presumably under the impression that Thompson had observation posts there. In fact, they were not once used for this purpose.

It was a day of rumours at the Bridge, of high hopes dashed by the non-appearance of any relieving force. Sometimes it was the 1st and 3rd Battalions who were coming through, then the South Staffords and the 11th. The Germans rolled forward more tanks and began a policy of demolition in order to dislodge the stubborn parachutists. Houses collapsed into rubble; some blazed. Surprisingly in such an inferno the number of killed was not forbiddingly high but the number of wounded was already a serious problem not only for the two overworked medical officers but also for Frost. As commander he was forced to the agonizing conclusion that there was no way of evacuating the wounded. They were placed in the vast cellars beneath the HQ building along with some 140 German prisoners, including SS men. Among those brought in was a young SS officer who said under interrogation that he had been sent to blow up the Bridge. He had pressed the plunger and nothing had happened. It was assumed from this information that the blaze on the bridge might have burned out the leads to the charges. In fact, however, Model had ordered that no bridges were to be blown.

In the close fighting, there was much use of the bayonet. During one encounter, Major Digby Tatham-Warter waved an umbrella as if it were a symbol of invincibility. On another occasion when the mortaring was heavy, he was seen shelter-ing under it. Here and there parties of parachutists stalked German tanks in the streets – some with Piat bombs, others with grenades. They developed some neat tricks. As a tank drove along a street, the men followed behind the houses until they were level with the tank and in position to fire Piats or throw gammon bombs.

Despite all their fevered aggression, the Germans had made little difference to Frost's positions by mid-afternoon. Frost and Gough discussed the likelihood of Gough and his Recce boys scalding across the Bridge at last light in order to try and force a link with XXX Corps, with whom they were now in contact.

Frost finally decided against the idea.

He was still optimistic about ultimate relief and so were those about him. During one lull, it was thought that a relieving force had got through from our own division and Frost's men made a megaphone out of wallpaper and called in strong English language to the unfortunately non-existent men down the road.

The Bridge was still intact. And as they looked into the area from which the rest of the division might emerge, it seemed to Frost and Gough that the whole of Arnhem was going up in flames and smoke. Two churches were well alight, their outlines like a frieze against the dull glow and the billowing smoke. They prepared for the morning, watchful and hopefully minimizing the significance of the light before their eyes.

In the divisional area the KOSBs, who had been fighting under Hackett, arrived. I put them in position north of Divisional HQ just below the railway line, between the Recce Squadron and Boy Wilson's Independent Company.

At midnight, I surveyed the strength returns which had just come in. Of those elements with which we were in contact, 3rd Battalion was down to forty men, the 1st to 116, the 11th to 150, and the South Staffords to 100. Also with us were a sizeable number of glider pilots fighting as infantry. Hackett had 250 officers and men of the 10th Battalion and 270 of the 156th. To the west the Border Regiment was dug in.

Though the day had gone against us, we realized that worse might come unless XXX Corps were to put in an appearance. An uneasy quiet settled in the area, broken by the occasional

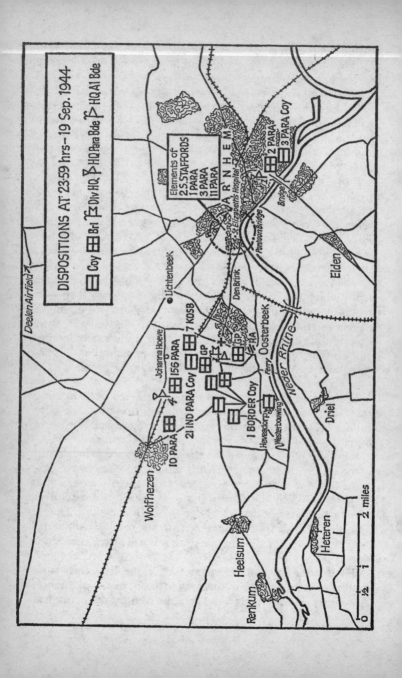

DISPOSITIONS AT 23·59 hrs – 19 Sep. 1944

⊞ Coy  ⊞ Bri  ⊠ Div HQ  ⊠ HQ Para Bde  ⊳ HQ A1 Bde

Elements of
2 S. STAFFORDS
1 PARA
3 PARA
11 PARA

ARNHEM

3 PARA Coy
2 PARA
Bridge
St. Elizabeth's Hospital
Pontoon Bridge
Elden

Lichtenbeek
Den Brink
7 KOSB
Johanna Hoeve
156 PARA
GP
RA
21 IND PARA Coy
GP
RA
Oosterbeek
1 BORDER Coy
Ferry
Heveadorp
Westerbouwing
Neder Rhine
Driel

10 PARA
Wolfhezen

Deelen Airfield

Heelsum
Renkum

Hetern

0  ½  1  2 miles

burst of small-arms fire and muffled explosions. Couriers and Resistance men went about their business and men kept vigil while their comrades attempted to sleep. And so it was to the east and west, while to the north Hackett on this fateful night organized his brigade for a march at first light into the divisional area. In the early hours, I received a signal from Corps HQ requesting a fresh dropping zone for the main force of Sosabowski's Polish Brigade. The only possible one now was south of the river near Driel, and this was duly passed to Corps.

With the drizzling dawn of Wednesday, September 20th, came the heaviest mortar stonk yet. Four officers were killed at Pip Hicks's HQ by a direct hit. In the hotel area fragments flew and the trees were smashed into a web of branches that littered the damp grounds where men kept their heads low in slit trenches covered with earth-filled re-supply containers. I contacted Hackett over the R/T shortly after 7.30 am and asked him to try to reach Divisional HQ as soon as he could, but he explained that he would be delayed as his entire brigade was engaged. Taken on frontally and on both flanks, he had already been compelled to alter his line of advance only to find the enemy in some strength on the alternative route. 'We have a certain number of tanks among us,' he said meaningly. It needed little imagination to understand his plight. And the information to hand from other sources showed that, except for the 2nd Battalion at the Bridge, the 1st Parachute Brigade had to all intents and purposes been wiped out. The South Staffords had ceased to exist as a unit, and the 11th Battalion had disintegrated. I knew that whatever prospects there had been of reaching Frost at the Bridge were now gone.

It was an awful conclusion to come to: it meant the abandonment of those men at the Bridge who had endured the most terrible battering. But with the weak force now left, I could no more hope to reinforce Frost than reach Berlin. Clearly, the Germans now controlled every route into the town and Bridge. They were being strengthened almost hourly, and their Tiger tanks were causing havoc. Already the best part of four battalions in the town had ceased to exist.

I had visualized the 4th Brigade coming through the divisional area, reorganizing, and then carrying out an offensive towards the Bridge. This was now impossible. I therefore ordered Hackett to forget the ultimate idea of pressing into the town, but to bring his brigade, or that part of it which survived, into position on the north-east side of our area. At all costs now we had to concentrate on holding a perimeter which would form a small bridgehead north of the Neder Rhine once XXX Corps caught up with us. It was essential now to save what we had left. Such was the situation when I was called to the phone shortly after 8 am.

'Hello, Sunray,' said a cheerful voice.

Suspicious because of the stories which were circulating about the Germans' messages on our signal net – 'We've got your Sunray,' they had once transmitted to Boy Wilson – I said: 'Can you give me an inkling who you are?'

There was a pause, then: 'It's the man who goes in for funny weapons.'

I thought of several characters who were so disposed in the 1st Airborne Division, and who were always prepared to try out for quality any lethal equipment. The caller was conscious of the possibility that eavesdroppers might be on the line – an open one through the public telephone system – and he now added, mysteriously: 'The man who is always late for your "O" groups.' Now I recalled the berating I had administered to Freddie Gough about his unpunctuality when I had given out my orders for Operation 'Market Garden'.

'My goodness,' I said, 'I thought you were dead.'

Briefly, Gough explained why he had been prevented from contacting me before and gave me a broad picture of the situation at the Bridge. I told him to pass on my personal congratulations on a fine effort to everyone concerned and then gave him to understand, as best I could without going into detail, that the rest of the division was in poor shape. 'I'm afraid,' I said, 'you can only hope for relief from the south. For the moment we can only try to preserve what we have left.'

Already the Germans, resuming their attacks, were forcing

a tightening of Frost's perimeter and the few houses held on the east side of the Bridge approach were being given up. 'It's pretty grim,' Gough said. 'We'll do what we can.'

I wished him the best of luck.

# CHAPTER FIVE

ON THIS morning of September 20th, the battle reached new levels of intensity as the Germans' retaliation was stepped up. A lot of stuff was flying about. The hotel was becoming very battered: outside there lay the corpses of men still to be buried, smashed vehicles, shellpits and holes in the ground in which men hardened themselves for what was still to come. They had dug slit trenches under the beech trees, and out among the laurel bushes; trees had been uprooted and signal cables zig-zagged between the hotel and the strange building like a tower in the grounds where Robert Loder-Symonds had his artillery HQ. Beyond this and a cluster of evergreens was a POW cage which we had found ready-made – the hotel tennis courts. And away beyond this immediate vista, the remnants of the division were fighting desperately. I had further news from the Bridge that the 2nd Battalion was under continuous fire and tank attacks, and that the whole Bridge area was devastated. To the north, Hackett had run into serious opposition as he attempted to pull back his 4th Brigade to join us, and the Germans had launched simultaneous attacks on the Independent Company and the Border Regiment. In the divisional area the shelling and mortaring was thick and violent at times, between quite long intervals of relative quiet.

As I thought out how we might at least succeed in holding a bridgehead north of the river, albeit not at the place originally intended, I wondered what could be keeping XXX Corps. Everywhere I went in the hotel and in the grounds beyond I was asked the same question: 'When is the 2nd Army coming?' I had not the slightest idea when they were likely to reach the south bank, though I knew that every effort was probably being made to relieve us. This was the first Division I had commanded and I had developed a very strong attachment to it: there was a wonderful spirit. And now I was having to see it cut about literally before my eyes. Although I was naturally disturbed by the non-arrival of

Horrocks's Corps, I was much more annoyed at the disappointingly meagre offensive air support we were receiving. The re-supply boys' gallantry had been magnificent, but our fighters were rare friends. We needed the Typhoons and Tempests to carry out rocket attacks on the Germans' gun and mortar positions. I knew nothing of the shortcomings on the air side, and there never has been a convincing explanation of what went wrong. For a while we were enduring this battering, the pilots of the 2nd Tactical Air Force, the fighter force on the Continent who knew the terrain almost as well as the south of England, were kept out of the battle zone for long periods. And no direct signals link was arranged between either the RAF HQ controlling the operation or Brereton's Allied Airborne Army HQ, and 2nd Tactical Air Force, with depressing consequences on at least one occasion.

In the hotel we now moved the operations room into the cellars. It was a tight squeeze. Down the aisle running through the main wine cellar, an arched dungeon from which coal was moved to make room for us, we had the ops table laid out with maps. A duty officer sat close up against it in order to make room for others to move between his chair and a roof support. My place was in the right-hand corner of the cellar between one of the blocked-up ground-level window grilles and a wine rack. Next to me was an officer of the Phantom Reconnaissance Unit, who had a direct wireless link to the War Office; then the chief clerk. On the far side of the cellar in a four-feet-deep recess leading to the other grille which overlooked the gravel path outside were several strangers, including two RAF officers who had been shot down during the re-supply operations.

By now, the overpopulated hotel and its grounds were taking on the more objectionable aspects of such confined fighting. Everyone had been living and sleeping in the same clothes since we landed, and as the Germans had long since cut off our water supplies, the lack of washing facilities meant we all got distinctly smelly. There were only two lavatories in the hotel, both of which were blocked. As they could not be flushed either, we were forced to use the grounds where proper latrines were out of the question. It was more than slightly disturbing to be caught in the open on such occasions by the odd shell and mortar bomb.

As this bitter day dragged on, with its numbing mortar and artillery attacks, Frost continued to hold out at the Bridge, Dickie Lonsdale and his scratch garrison kept up their guerrilla activities in the south-east, the Border Regiment was pre-occupied to the west and Hackett, fighting his way out with the 4th Brigade, lost contact with us. For a time, I knew nothing of the fate of this force. In fact, although surrounded and subjected to fire from ahead and on the flanks, the brigade – or rather, what was left of it – was, as Hackett reported, 'handling beautifully'. Many of the troops, out of ammunition and even weapons, were using captured German rifles and automatics. In a bid to increase the pace Hackett changed the line of advance from a south-easterly direction to an easterly one, bringing the 10th Battalion through to spearhead the advance while the 156th Battalion, which had been stopped, took up the rearguard. Its commanding officer, Lieutenant-Colonel Sir Richard des Voeux, had been killed. One of the officers with Hackett, Lieutenant-Colonel Derick Heathcoat-Amory, who was a casualty, was strapped to a stretcher on a jeep which was also carrying mortar bombs. It was set alight by a German flame-thrower and somehow Heathcoat-Amory was released just in time. Hackett's brigade major, Bruce Dawson, shot a German with a rifle and soon after-wards Hackett followed suit. Then Dawson was shot through the head and killed. As they entered the woods, the two battalions were subjected to substantial small-arms fire which raked the rides between the tall trees. Impatient about the rate of progress, Hackett now sent orders to the 10th Battalion urging them to 'pull the plug out'.

They fixed bayonets.

I saw the remains of the battalion as it turned off the main road, following the line of trees into the HQ area. The men were exhausted, filthy, and bleeding; their discipline was immaculate. The memory of their arrival has remained strongly with me. Their commander, Lieutenant-Colonel Ken Smyth, his right arm bandaged where a bullet had struck, reported breathlessly: 'We have been heavily taken on, sir. I have sixty men left.'

'What has happened to Hackett?' I asked.

'He'll be here as soon as they can disengage,' said Smyth. 'They were in rather a mess in the woods up there.'

It was 1.30 pm. I could no longer contemplate putting Smyth and the survivors into the original position I had in mind in the 4th Brigade, and I told them to cover the cross-roads to the north-east of the Divisional HQ area. The three-score men trooped away under the screen of trees to take over several houses which straddled the crossroads. Many of them were killed there, and Smyth, who was half buried in one of the houses, was later to die in hospital.

They gave no ground to the end.

Meantime, Hackett with the 156th Battalion had been unable to keep up with the 10th. Even as Smyth was reporting to me, Hackett and his men were confronted by smock-attired soldiers standing openly at the head of the rides through the wood. 'Come on, Tommy,' the soldiers called. 'Come on.' In the half light of the woods, which the extremely warm autumn had left late in full leaf, the soldiers could not be properly identified; but it seemed certain that they were Poles. Otherwise, why stand out in full view like that? The British paratroopers emerged, relieved at this support. They were met by Spandaus, and men died with greetings half shouted on their tongues. The Germans took cover in a depression and Hackett ordered that they should be rooted out. Using bayonets, the parachutists made quick work of this and Hackett, after the clash, moved into the hollow to collect his depleted band. He had about thirty men from the 156th, a dozen from the 10th, another dozen from his own HQ, and a score or more others – and seven officers. Presently, others found their way to the hollow where now about 100 men were congregated. Here, Hackett resolved to stay until dusk.

All through the afternoon, the Germans kept up their harrying tactics. Whenever they approached within grenade throwing distance of the hollow, they were seen off by the bayonet. In one counter-attack from the hollow, Hackett and a number of others came out with rifles and bayonets to silence a machine-gun sited thirty yards away which had been making life unbearable for the beleaguered force. A number of Germans were killed and Hackett himself came upon the machine-gun, unmanned now, its barrel hot to the touch. He glanced into a nearby slit trench and there saw a German cowering in terror, his head pressed down in the sandy soil. In a long moment, Hackett paused. He saw the cloth of the German's tunic stretched tight between two sharp, thin shoulder-blades; the pathetic helplessness of the man was too much for Hackett. He could not bring himself to use his bayonet.

There was more German activity now and Hackett had to recall his party. Within three minutes, the gun they had over-run and whose crew-member Hackett had spared, was firing again. Some Mark I tanks were brought up to harass the British who stalked them with plastic bombs only to find German infantrymen in wait. In this fighting, Hackett noticed the zest of his chief clerk, a sergeant called Dudley Pearson.

In the hollow there were many casualties now, and the last of the medical officers had earlier stayed behind with other wounded.

By the way their attacks were increasing, the Germans were bent on liquidating the position before nightfall. At 4.30 in the afternoon, therefore, Hackett decided that his force would have to make a break for it. They steeled themselves for the vital moment. Hackett, who had been using a German weapon, now exchanged it for a British rifle with an officer who had been hit in the hand.

The parachutists broke cover.

With fixed bayonets, they charged out suddenly, and only a few men were lost. They kept going, and about half a mile farther on, they were astonished to find themselves in a comparative haven – the beautifully dug positions of the Border Regiment on the west side of the evolving perimeter.

Hackett came on and reported to me. He had seventy

officers and men. The time was 6.50 pm. Together with some sixty sappers of the 4th Parachute Squadron who had been fighting on a different approach, Hackett's men took up position south of the 10th Battalion. Hackett set up his Brigade HQ in the wooded part of the hotel grounds, some fifty yards from my own HQ. I said to him: 'Take a night's rest.'

We were now in no condition to attempt any sort of offensive towards the town. I told Hackett that we must at all costs now hold this perimeter on the northern bank and not allow ourselves to be destroyed. Naturally, his first request was for information about the progress of XXX Corps.

Our wireless communications with the outside world, and especially with Browning's HQ, were still practically non-existent; but two signal links were still functioning well – the BBC war correspondent's set, and Phantom reporting unit. Working one of these powerful long-distance sets in his square yard of cellar space next to me, the Phantom officer suddenly laid down his headphones and came up with the exciting information shortly after two o'clock in the afternoon that the Guards Armoured Division was fighting in the Nijmegen area and preparing to rush the bridge over the Waal. And at this very moment seventy Dakotas droned slowly across the battlefield dropping supply panniers. I ordered that news of the impending Guards bid should be made known to everyone in the division. It was heartening stuff, and I personally conveyed it to some of the troops myself as I went out into the grounds and around the defence posts. They needed a tonic.

In the sky was a second reminder that we had not been overlooked and the men in their slit trenches were inspired. We had tried to get messages back by every means to prevent the airmen from dropping their loads in the scheduled places which were in German hands. We had sent co-ordinates of the places where they should try to put the stuff down. Hopefully, as the Dakotas came on, we watched for the first signs that the pilots were aware, by order or by observation, of the situation. Again, the ground signals were laid and lit, and the troops held out parachute silks. But the aircraft kept to the planned dropping points and the Germans again found themselves receiving gifts from their enemies. Only the overs reached us. Some crews, overshooting, came round in face of most appalling flak. Some aircraft were on fire. Hundreds of us saw one man in the doorway of a blazing Dakota refusing to release a pannier until he had found the exact spot, though the machine was a flaming torch now and he had no hope of escape.

During the hectic and confused afternoon, I tried to maintain physical contact with as many of the units in the perimeter as I could, partly in the hope that my presence might help morale and also because I wanted to get the picture absolutely right. On one of my trips, I went to to see Boy Wilson and his Independent Company who held a number of houses in a heavily wooded district. I wanted to see how he was doing and also to warn him of Hackett's possible appearance in the Independent Company's area from the north. I took my ADC, Graham Roberts, and we were given directions by some troops which led us along a wooded ride. Suddenly we found ourselves in the middle of a vigorous dispute between the Independent Company and a number of SS men. From slit trenches on the roadside, faces appeared and men shouted and gesticulated. I braked hard, and, with Roberts, made an undignified dive into a ditch.

We had run between the lines: the ride was a No Man's Land.

As little was to be gained from staying put, I decided to make a run for it to the house occupied by Wilson some fifty yards away on a slight wooded rise. I told Roberts of my intention, and told him to collect the jeep if he could. We ventured out simultaneously. I reached the house without being molested, but Roberts attracted some enemy attention when he climbed into the jeep. The ride was too narrow to allow him to turn round, so he decided to drive on towards a right-hand turn which looped round close to the house. Going fast, he negotiated the corner and swerved to avoid a burned-out German half-track. Something must have hit the jeep, for the steering suddenly collapsed. The jeep careered into a tree and was wrecked. Roberts was thrown clear and rolled into a ditch. He shook himself and heard disembodied voices calling advice. From the undergrowth around him came the call: 'For God's sake get out of it! Snipers!' He had a severe pain in his leg, but in desperation he managed to jump over a four-and-a-half-feet high wire-mesh fence. When he arrived at the house, he had a large swelling on his forehead as well as a leg injury and I sent him off to the RAP for attention. More than anything he was worried about my jeep. 'I'm afraid, sir,' he said sadly, 'that it's a complete write off.'

Roberts went off and was presently tended by Graeme Warrack, who was having a hectic time. During the early mortar stonk on Divisional HQ an American wireless operator was badly hurt in the stomach and Warrack had personally conveyed him to the dressing station at the Hotel Schoonhord, and then found himself in the midst of a battle. It was turning out to be that sort of operation. Mortar bombs fell among the medical transport, a Dutch civilian car was hit on the road, and a six-pounder was contesting the issue with a German self-propelled gun. A few minutes later, Warrack heard German orders being given in the street. He ripped off his badges of rank and went upstairs to tend the wounded. Soon, those who could walk were marched off with some RAMC personnel. Then the dressing station got a direct hit and Warrack and others found themselves removing wounded men who had now been wounded a second time. As the dust began to settle, two more shells crashed into the building, which later was festooned with Red Cross flags with a particularly large one on the roof. A German officer called to inquire about the German wounded being treated there, one of whom, a young Nazi, refused treatment for a shattered knee for four hours until the pain became too great and he consented to the British tending him.

When I heard that the dressing station had been overrun, I sent Major John Royle, second-in-command of a wing of the Glider Pilot Regiment, to find out what was happening. He was killed in the middle of the road at the dressing station. At one time before the war, Royle had been a regular subaltern in the Highland Light Infantry. On the outbreak of war he joined up in the ranks and became a warrant officer in the Scots Guards. Later, he was commissioned into the Glider Pilot Regiment. However fatalistic it is possible to get in the matter of casualties, one cannot but be sad when these are caused as a direct result of a personal order.

Throughout this day, wounded were filling the dressing stations. There now began a remarkable situation as officers and men went for attention to a dressing station guarded by Germans and then returned to their own lines to continue the fight. This strange state of affairs was to exist for days. On this fateful Wednesday, however, some of the walking wounded were taken away as prisoners. Surgery went on all day long. A soldier with a badly shattered foot was prepared for an amputation when it was discovered that the only amputation saws were with other surgeons at the Hotel Taffelburg, another dressing station still within our own lines. It was decided to use an escape file. This was cleaned and sterilized and a piece of wire was run through one end. Forceps were used to grip the other end, and the instrument was worked like a two-handed saw. In a few minutes they had cut through the tibia.

At the Schoonhord, Warrack and his colleagues had learned that it was unsafe to venture too near the windows because of the German snipers, who were somewhat trigger happy. The Germans themselves appeared to have few men to spare, for they left as guard on the dressing station a very jittery soldier with an automatic. A British lance-corporal who had once been runner-up in the Army middleweight championships was detailed to keep an eye on him.

In mid-afternoon, as the attrition continued and our supply situation worsened, I sent off a signal saying:

Enemy attacking main bridge in strength. Situation serious for 1 Para Brigade. Enemy also attacking position east from Heelsum and west from Arnhem. Situation serious but an forming close perimeter defence round Hartenstein with remainder of Div. Relief essential both areas earliest possible. Still retain ferry crossing Heveadorp.

Our communications were still a tremendous handicap,

and there is some evidence that this signal did not finally get through until the following morning, Thursday September 21st.

As dusk came over the battlefield, a plan was made as a forlorn hope to get supplies through to Frost's battalion at the Bridge. Three Bren carriers were loaded with ammunition and other sorely needed gear, and now they set out to run the gauntlet. In the covering darkness, one scorched through the forward German positions and was last heard racing into the town, a second was hit by an 88-mm shell, and the third was forced to turn back. Lieutenant Heaps, the peripatetic Canadian, was with this party which tried to get through, but even this determined young man failed to make it.

At the Bridge, the survivors of Frost's force were suffering from a shortage of ammunition – the six-pounder shells were almost done, and there were about ten Piat shots left between the men still fighting – and were being pressed without respite. Earlier in the day, soon after he had spoken to me on the telephone, Gough had taken over command when Frost was badly wounded in the leg, though he continued to refer major decisions to Frost. By now, the Germans were describing Frost as 'the mad Colonel', a nick-name which stuck later when the Germans told their own people over the radio about the operation. Tatham-Warter, whose influence on morale at the Bridge had proved incalculable, now took over the remnants of the 2nd Battalion. Lieutenant Grayburn, who had been wounded in the shoulder, led a succession of patrols among the Germans after the tanks had set fire to houses, thereby forcing the paratroopers to abandon their positions. They reformed and on several occasions took back places from which the German armour had originally driven them. Once, Grayburn kept the Germans preoccupied while a party of sappers removed the fuses from demolition charges which the Germans had laid under the bridge pylons. Shortly after 5 pm I received a signal from the Bridge stating, 'It may not be possible for the Germans to destroy the Bridge.' Grayburn was again wounded during this phase and later in the evening he was killed by fire from a tank. He was awarded a posthumous Victoria Cross.

In the basement of the big warehouse building at the Bridge, the medical officers and orderlies were trying to cope with some two hundred wounded, many of them serious cases. And outside, among the houses, the fighting could not have been closer. It is easy to imagine the chagrin of the defenders as four Tiger tanks and an armoured-car were able to cross the Bridge with impunity. In order to fulfil Bittrich's order to re-take the Bridge, the Germans suffered many casualties: it had been an expensive business for them. There was hardly a building in the Bridge area that had not been badly hit or burnt. It was a scene of devastation. And now the Germans, who were using phosphorus shells, set the big building on fire. It was in danger of collapse. The two doctors, Logan and Wright, informed Gough that he had the option of surrendering the wounded or having them burned alive in the cellars. There was no question of choice. Two of the medical personnel presently walked out with a Red Cross flag and arranged for the removal of the wounded. This was agreed, and both sides held their fire as the Germans began to collect the wounded men. The paratroopers still in action moved back while the removal progressed. Then Gough and his companions saw the Germans were coming right into their positions and moving towards the jeeps that were still intact. Gough ordered that they were not to come any closer. 'We cannot remove your wounded unless we use your jeeps,' came the German reply.

Gough had no counter to this ultimatum.

The work went on.

When the wounded were out of the way, the shooting started again.

An attempt was made to break out westwards towards the divisional area but the move was spotted before they had covered fifty yards: some were killed, others wounded. Those who still fought were outnumbered, surrounded, without food and water, and had little ammunition left.

They were no more than fugitives among the dust and the rubble.

The rest of the division strengthened their positions around the perimeter. It was a confused, uneasy night. Payton-Reid and one of his company commanders, Gordon Sheriff, were discussing the KOSB layout in the grounds of the White House, a country hotel around which they had taken position after their move south of the railway, when they became aware of a soldier standing beside them in the gloom.

'Well,' Payton-Reid demanded. 'What do you want?'

To the astonishment of the two officers, the reply was in German and Sheriff, a strongly-built, former rugby player, went for the man's throat and they fell together. Payton-Reid was unable to shoot as they rolled over for fear of hitting Sheriff. In his death throes, the German hurled a stick bomb which exploded without wounding either of the officers.

They were walking away when out of the darkness came a gurgling wail. 'We'd better go back and put him out of his misery,' Payton-Reid said, and the two of them returned.

The German, however, was dead. The wail came from a goat which someone had killed for food.

The grounds of the White House were shortly to become the scene of much bitter fighting and Payton-Reid, knowing what was probably in store, was still mulling over the embarrassing incident which had occurred on their arrival. With his second-in-command, he had gone up the hotel drive and knocked at the door. At that time the area was peaceful with not a German in sight. The Dutchman who answered them had fallen on them with unrestrained delight. He led them into the dining-room where they were fêted by staff and guests as liberators. Toasts were offered. And even when Payton-Reid announced that his men would be taking up position around the building, the reaction was that of over-joyed relief. 'I felt like a hypocrite,' he told me later. He could not bring himself to stop their premature celebrations. In the grounds was an air-raid shelter which was converted into a battle HQ. A stock of wine was discovered, and this helped to offset the water shortage. As there was much more red wine than white, the officer in charge of the stock tried to induce a colleague who had asked for white to accept red instead.

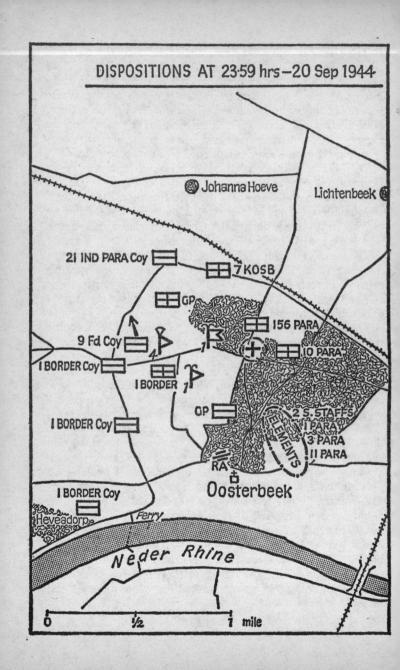

DISPOSITIONS AT 23·59 hrs – 20 Sep 1944

Johanna Hoeve

Lichtenbeek

21 IND PARA Coy

7 KOSB

GP

156 PARA

9 Fd Coy

10 PARA

I BORDER Coy

I BORDER

GP

I BORDER Coy

2 S. STAFFS
ELEMENTS
I PARA
3 PARA
11 PARA

RA

I BORDER Coy

Oosterbeek

Heveadorp

Ferry

Neder Rhine

0        ½        1 mile

'No thanks,' said the other rather offhandedly. 'I personally prefer white.'

The Germans were observing their usual ritual of quieting their guns at night and getting their snipers into positions. I walked round the HQ defence positions and noted the eerie, ominous hush which had settled everywhere. Here and there men came from their slit trenches to exercise themselves. An occasional dispatch rider nosily drove into the hotel approach. In the hotel, the duty officer perused a signal from Corps HQ with the news we had been waiting to hear: the bridge at Nijmegen had been captured intact and our armour was moving towards us. And at 1.15 am I was awakened with further news that the Guards Armoured Division had been ordered to go flat out for the Arnhem Bridge at first light. In fact, the efforts to reach us had been distinguished by one of the most vividly daring acts of the war and marred by an incomprehensible succession of examples of casualness and lack of urgency. During the afternoon of Wednesday, September 20th, the 504th US Parachute Regiment launched their assault boats into the fast-running Waal a mile downstream from the Nijmegen road bridge. Only about half the boats of the first wave reached the north bank, but 200 paratroopers swam and swarmed ashore and they were gradually reinforced.

It was an incredible feat of arms, for the river was turbulent, the north bank was defended and they had nearly a quarter of a mile of water to cross.

By 6.30 pm the Americans were moving towards the road bridge, having already taken the northern end of the railway bridge. In Nijmegen, the Grenadier Guards and a battalion of Jim Gavin's 82nd US Division had cleared the approaches – the Valkhof and Huner Park – and at 7 pm five British tanks pressed on through the park, taking on some German guns, and then clanked over the bridge. Two of them were hit by anti-tank guns stationed on the bridge, but another two kept going, demolishing a road block at the northern end. They linked up with the Americans now, and the long flat road with its rust-coloured setts lay ahead – to Arnhem.

In this bridgehead – they paused.

Later in the evening, Boy Browning drove across the

bridge and found the Guards held up. He met two Guards officers there and asked how things were going.

'The leading Irish Guards tanks have been knocked out and they're blocking the road,' one of the officers replied.

'Can't you get off the road?' Browning asked.

'We can't. There is an eight feet drop either side.'

Browning had been given cause to remind the spearheads of XXX Corps that they still had some way to go, and he certainly had the feeling that they lacked the right sense of urgency. If the Guards Armoured Division had been on time, he felt sure he could have secured the bridge with their leading group and a US combat team forty-eight hours earlier. There was a further complication: when the bridge at Nijmegen was eventually captured the 43rd Division who were to come up to us were only at Grave, having been held up in transit by most serious transport jams on the single road running up the corridor.

I knew nothing of this during Wednesday.

As Horrocks planned to attack north from the Nijmegen bridgehead – he ordered the Guards Armoured to move 'as early as possible and at maximum speed' – the last British resistance at the Arnhem Bridge was being overcome. In the grey morning light, the Germans began to winkle out the gallant fugitives. From cellars on opposite sides of one ruined street, the crews of light automatics, one British, the other German, had been fighting it out. As their ammunition ran down, the British held their fire for longer spells. Then came a final burst and the awed Germans saw two very young paratroopers emerge from the cellar. While the leading man attempted to draw the German crew's fire, the other followed up with a knife. Both were wounded and, as they fell, the German machine-gunner stopped firing and changed position to cut off their retreat. A German officer later described this incident to me as 'something which impressed the battle-hardened German troops because it was not spontaneous but obviously thought out'.

It was possibly the last act of resistance at the Bridge.

Gough ordered a wounded RASC officer, David Clark, to give himself up with the rest of the casualties to the first

Germans who appeared. German infantry were now scouring the houses and rubble heaps. As they came nearer, Clark refused to surrender. 'You're a pretty strong chap,' he said to Gough. 'You could carry me pick-a-back.' The searchers were lobbing grenades into house windows and doorways as a final inducement to the evaders. Gough scrambled beneath a stack of logs. He heard the approach of jackboots. Hardly daring to breathe, he suddenly felt his left foot being pulled and he was dragged in a shower of timber into a circle of grey-uniformed soldiers who all looked as if they were in their 'teens. Looking up into these impossibly young faces, he burst out laughing.

When they had left England, Frost and his men hoped that the Bridge would only have to be held for twenty-four hours before XXX Corps came through. They had held it against some of Bittrich's best soldiers from the 9th and 10th SS Panzer Divisions for three days and four nights and it was not long enough. For no further move had yet been made out of the Nijmegen bridgehead. And as daylight showed up the great Bridge of Arnhem tanks were moving across it – south, past a mound of German dead.

At nine o'clock on Thursday morning I held a divisional conference at which I announced that the defence of the perimeter would be divided into two commands, east and west, with Hackett and Hicks respectively in control. On the west Hicks would have the remnants of three companies of the Border Regiment, the surviving KOSBs who were holding the northern edge, the Independent Company and a miscellany of Poles, glider pilots and sappers. Hackett had the remnants of the 10th and 156th Battalions, Sheriff Thompson's 1st Light Regiment, the Lonsdale Force consisting of the survivors of the 1st, 3rd and 11th Parachute Battalions and South Staffords, a handful of 2nd Parachute Battalion troops who had never got to the Bridge, and some glider pilots. From all sides I heard the glider pilots were performing magnificently as infantry and were certainly not the liability that some glider pilots had been in other airborne operations. In this respect, we were one up on the Americans; for even in the crack 82nd US Airborne Division the glider pilots were not trained to look after themselves once they were on the ground, and Jim Gavin was subsequently to remark on the handicap they were to prove in the fighting.

In the horseshoe-shaped perimeter I now had some 3000 men, and in the heart of the area Sheriff Thompson's Light Regiment had gun batteries sited north-east and north-west of Oosterbeek Church on the rising ground. All through, these men had displayed a remarkably high standard of efficiency and marksmanship. Following the conference, I visited the 1st Battery's command post with Robert Loder-Symonds just at the time when Captain Macmillan announced with some relish that he had at last contacted the outside artillery by radio. Loder-Symonds himself went on to speak and there were a few exchanges which suggested that the 2nd Army artillery unit at the other end were suspicious about our identity. German wireless trespassing was a common feature in the operations and the outside artillery commander, who knew him personally, now asked Loder-Symonds to give the name of his wife.

'Merlin,' Loder-Symonds replied.

It was not enough. 'What is your wife's favourite sport?'

'Falconry,' said Loder-Symonds.

Normally, 2nd Army would not have listened to our calls because we did not know the current callsigns; now, however, they could not do too much for us. I called on Hackett and Hicks at their headquarters and told them to select targets for the 64th Medium Regiment when it got within range. Thus started one of the most exciting and remarkable artillery shoots I have ever experienced. From a range of about eleven miles, these gunners proceeded to answer our calls with a series of shoots on targets nominated by Loder-Symonds, some of which were not more than a hundred yards out from our perimeter line. It involved certain risks, but the situation merited their being taken, and in the afternoon the shelling had had quite noticeable effect on the Germans. Hearing the whine and the tremendous blast of these medium shells – there is surely no more terrifying noise in war – we felt glad the 64th were on our side. And now, supported by a battery of heavies, these gunners broke up several attacks supported by self-propelled guns on the eastern flank.

Inside the perimeter, snipers were an embarrassment. I encountered several small parties, led by divisional officers whose expected functions on the administrative side had never matured, going out on sniper hunts. Some of these were successful, but one particularly ambitious German who had stationed himself in the tall beeches behind the headquarters was making the approaches to the rear door dangerous. Already he had hit a few troops and I saw Pip Hicks, who was only a few days short of forty-nine, coming across the sniper's range at an astonishing speed.

During the morning, the German mortaring was especially heavy in the Light Regiment's area and around Divisional HQ. Suddenly, there was a loud rending explosion and it was seen that our ammunition dump on the open common across the main road had been hit, and was now going up in a series of crackling roars. As much material as possible was salvaged and brought nearer the hotel. Three jeeps were on fire. Any sort of vehicle would soon be almost useless anyway; for the roads and open ground were now littered with the increasing debris of battle – fallen trees, shattered transport and rubble. Our best hope now was that the 64th Medium would give us enough support to contain the Germans until the Guards Armoured Division and whatever infantry they had with them caught up with us. Already the shelling had put new heart into the troops; nothing succeeds like the big guns in building infantry morale.

I had noticed on my morning tour of our positions that the collection and treatment of casualties was proving a heavy burden to those in the area, and on my return I told Graeme Warrack that he ought to check up. He went off in a jeep. Another spell of heavy mortaring began and soon afterwards Charles Mackenzie reported that the two hundred-odd German prisoners in the tennis courts were complaining of being unnecessarily exposed to the mortaring and were quoting Geneva Conventions. I went down with Mackenzie and an interpreter and addressed them. As they lined up, I saw that they had been pretty badly shaken. Around the tennis courts stood the Military Police and glider pilots with Stens under their arms; the prisoners, in shabby uniforms and with weary, bearded faces, stood in sullen silence on the pitted courts where already a number of mortar bombs had burst.

They were hardly in worse case than my own men who were being blasted by tree bursts which scattered metal fragments far more widely than a ground hit. Glancing up and down the lines, I said: 'We expect you to behave in the way that British soldiers have to behave in conditions such as this. We will do everything possible to enable you to dig in. As for food, I know how you are feeling. But we have none ourselves, and you will get what is due to you as it becomes available.' I knew that once it is suggested to a German that he is not as good as someone else, he damn soon tries hard to prove that he is. When I left, the prisoners were being issued with several shovels to dig through the hard surface of the courts. Others used mess tins to scoop away the gravel and soil.

The pressure on the perimeter continued, but it was spasmodic and tended to be staggered between areas, and none of the attacks was made at much more than company strength supported by a few tanks and self-propelled guns. While it was possible that the Germans were contenting themselves with our gradual liquidation under the hail of mortars and shells, I was surprised that at no time was an overall, co-ordinated attack ever attempted. At this point, the battle bore an odd characteristic of suspense which caused me to ponder the possibilities that the Germans had other ideas in their heads. The probing and pestering at a number of points was understandable if the Germans considered that their colleagues beyond the river had the slightest chance of stopping the main advance of the 2nd Army. I could not bring myself to accept that even the German senior officers nursed any such optimism.

The enemy was up against the time factor just as we were.

At this stage, I naturally knew nothing of Bittrich's theory that the best tactics were to hit us with a number of small, scattered actions because of the lack of initiative of British junior commanders and NCOs. In this assessment, Bittrich was working from an assumption which may have a basis of truth. Possibly our training has never allowed for enough responsibility to be given to junior officers and NCOs.

Nonetheless, I consider that the surrounding Germans had the capacity and the resources to come through us on Thursday, September 21st. One German staff car, to our immense chagrin, did drive straight through the main road running past the Hartenstein. With a concentrated attack, the Germans must soon have overwhelmed us; but the scattered small-scale attacks continued and these were held. First, Boy Wilson was under pressure; then it was the Border Regiment to the west and the KOSBs to the north who bore the brunt. There was also pressure on the eastern flank. Hackett's staff captain, an extremely cool young man called Jasper Booty, sat on the edge of his slit trench twirling a bullet-holed red beret round his finger and opined, 'You know, sir, the trouble with these bloody Germans is that they don't know what to do.'

Hackett was touring his kingdom. He called on Dickie Lonsdale and chatted briefly with Robert Cain, who was ultimately to win a Victoria Cross but who, at that moment, was temporarily stone deaf from the din. With Hackett was Tiny Maddon, his new brigade major who until that morning had been on my staff at Division. Together they visited the dressing station in the large, white-fronted house next to Oosterbeek Church and fronting the river. They spoke to the wounded and to Mrs Kate Ter Horst, a kindly Dutch woman who was helping the medical staff to care for the wounded while also looking after her own family of five young children, including a baby, in the cellar. Already her name was being mentioned whenever troops were gathered in the gunners' area and along the Oosterbeek road. After having a few words with Randall Martin, the doctor, who was known as 'Morph', Hackett and Maddon were crossing the front lawn of the house when a mortar-burst killed Maddon outright under the lone tree and chipped Hackett about the face and hands. Sheriff Thompson, who was near by, was also badly wounded. They cleaned up Hackett's wounds and took Thompson inside. Later, Hackett took temporary refuge in the gunners' HQ.

When he arrived in the same area, Warrack also stopped some splinters. Unsure which was the Ter Horst's house, he fetched up in another white house where he found three badly wounded Germans. He gave them morphia, tended their wounds, and then, stepping outside, came upon a British officer standing over a parachutist with a terrible head wound. Warrack quickly examined the soldier, who was in poor shape, and said, 'He'll die.' The officer cocked his .45 and momentarily Warrack was convinced that he intended to practise euthanasia. In fact, as he started to explain, the officer was merely preparing to escort the chief doctor to the casualty post. There, Warrack found Martin overwhelmed with work in a house packed tight with wounded and under almost constant fire. Sheriff Thompson had a bad stomach wound. A few feet away lay a German. Mrs Ter Horst, far from showing any resentment at the break-up of her home, was behaving with a graceful stoicism which was an inspiration to the wounded and those who tended them.

Three days before, Martin had driven up to the house in his jeep and asked for the use of some small place where he could treat casualties. 'We don't need much,' he said. 'Only the lightly wounded will be treated here and sent on to the hospital in the Taffelberg Hotel.' Then, opening his first-aid case, he had said optimistically: 'I hope we won't have many casualties.'

The medical unit took over the washhouse.

But soon the wounded lay all over the ground floor of the house, some on stretchers, others on the ground, and the medical bombardier had then been led upstairs by Mrs Ter Horst who indicated that he should help her take the mattresses and blankets off her beds for the wounded. He refused. 'We wouldn't want to spoil your fine things,' he said.

Whereupon she insisted and threw open the doors of the linen cupboard. The bedclothes were stacked ready for use but later the bombardier showed Mrs Ter Horst a bale of blankets which had come in with the re-supply aircraft. Mrs Ter Horst was moved by the determination of these airborne soldiers not to inconvenience her more than was absolutely necessary. They even refused to accept the food she offered them. Once during a lull in the mortaring she had gone outside and noticed a soldier lying between two jeeps. Anxiously, she touched his forehead. His eyes opened. 'I'm all right,' he assured her. 'I'd just gone off to sleep.'

And as the mortaring increased and the house shook under the blast, the tall slim Dutchwoman with the blonde hair and the calm ice-blue eyes was torn between her family of youngsters in the cellar and the badly hurt soldiers above. Somehow, she found the strength and will to satisfy both loyalties: she consoled the children in the cellar, putting them to sleep with a fairy tale, and then climbed the stairs to inspire and help the wounded.

During Warrack's visit, the congestion in the house was such that he arranged for a number of walking wounded to be led to the Taffelberg Hotel under a Red Cross flag. His own jeep had been wrecked near the church, and now he borrowed Martin's in order to take what he described as 'the most promising surgery cases' – two in the back, and two strapped across the bonnet. With the Red Cross flag flying, he put his foot down. When someone asked him whether such a bumping on a swaying jeep was really good for the patients, he answered: 'I don't consider it does them any good to tarry. Any slight shock they may suffer from a rapid journey is offset by the fact that they arrive in one piece.'

Twice in the afternoon the RAF tried to get supplies to us. Their first mission, at 12.45 pm, was disastrous. The aircraft were shot up by Me 109s before our eyes and there was some evidence to suggest that the Germans were using our signals to attract some of the supplies, and that they were operating at least one of our Eurekas. The second mission, at 4 pm, was much more successful and we acquired a small proportion of the sorely needed ammunition and rations as they fell. It was a costly day for the RAF, whose losses were twenty per cent of the aircraft taking part.

At 5.15 pm came the encouraging news that the Poles were arriving on their dropping zone south of the river just east of Driel. From the southern part of our perimeter, the spire of Driel Church was a solitary and prominent landmark in the flat land beyond the river. By now, however, the Heveadorp Ferry by which we might have got the Poles across had fallen into German hands and my chief engineer Eddie Myers was having little luck in gathering the boats and rafts necessary to ferry the Poles. He planned to use jeep trailers for the purpose and now dispatched one of his field squadrons to see what it could do.

The Poles' arrival produced a rapid reaction from the Germans who, besides contesting the landings fiercely, now put in strong attacks supported by tanks and self-propelled guns against the eastern flank of the perimeter and also made inroads against the KOSB positions to the north. Loder-Symonds called for a supporting shoot from the 64th Medium which smashed the German offensive on the eastern side, but the KOSBs, who had previously been subjected to intense mortaring, had to halt the Germans with the bayonet. They reoccupied their positions only at high cost and in the end were reduced to 150 all ranks.

In the heat and haze of battle, the Independent Company got the impression that the KOSBs had been wiped out, and there was some alarm when this report came through. What had happened was that the KOSBs had sidestepped a couple of houses to shorten their line. Even now there was a disconcerting stretch of open ground between them and the Independent Company. The line of houses held was not continuous and the KOSBs were in a somewhat dangerous spot. During the battle of the White House, their casualty clearing post had come in for some unpleasant attention and after one direct hit Devlin, medical officer in charge, considered that he ought to move back from the immediate battle zone. Payton-Reid warned him, however, that if the post were moved back, it could not be protected. 'Either back or front,' Payton-Reid explained solemnly, 'you are in No Man's Land.'

'It would be better than where we are now,' the MO insisted.

'Very well,' said Payton-Reid. 'We'll do all we can for you, but it will be difficult.'

Led by the MO and Payton-Reid's wounded second-in-command, Major Coke, those able to walk now set off for the new medical centre. As they approached a crossroads they were intercepted by a German patrol which was all set to fire when the MO held aloft the Red Cross flag. He and Coke went forward. The German commander, a very young and precise officer, demanded to know what it was all about.

'We're just going to our RAP,' Coke replied in understandable German.

'All I know is that you are in our territory,' said the young officer. 'You are therefore our prisoners.'

Coke, a small and dapper man who was never slow in thought or action, adopted an air of pained bravado. 'Oh, but you can't do that,' he said. 'We're under the Red Cross. You can't touch us.'

The German officer was now less certain than he had been of the correctness of his earlier statement.

'You just can't touch us,' Coke declared grandly. 'Run away home. We're going to *our* house.'

For a long moment it looked as if the German would see it Coke's way; then he saw a way out both for himself and this insistent Britisher who might well be right. 'I think you had better come and see my major,' he offered.

The two of them then left for the house which the Germans were using as their HQ. When Coke was produced and his theory explained, the major, who was longer in the tooth than the junior officer, thought it was one of the best jokes he had ever heard. 'They are our prisoners,' he told the younger officer. Coke, Devlin and the rest of the wounded were now told to proceed down the road leading into the heart of German-held territory. Presently, they came upon two German tanks moving towards the front. Imperiously Coke stood in the middle of the road and held up his hand. The tanks stopped and Coke entered into an animated discussion with the German officer in the leading tank. Then he smiled, the tanks turned round, and Coke beckoned the wounded troops to climb aboard. 'He's commandeered the bloody things,' one soldier said – and so he had. Coke, who came from a family which had produced generations of soldiers, was tragically killed some time after this episode when with

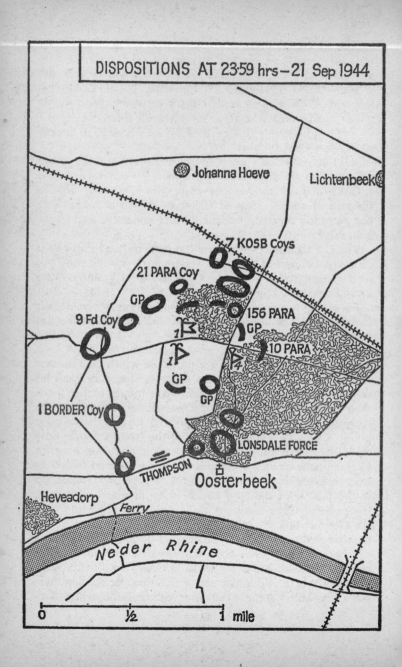

DISPOSITIONS AT 23·59 hrs – 21 Sep 1944

Johanna Hoeve

Lichtenbeek

7 KOSB Coys

21 PARA Coy

GP

9 Fd Coy

156 PARA

GP

10 PARA

GP

GP

1 BORDER Coy

LONSDALE FORCE

THOMPSON

Oosterbeek

Heveadorp

Ferry

Neder Rhine

0       ½       1 mile

characteristic enterprise he led a mass break-out of British prisoners.

Early in the evening, it was becoming clear that I would soon have to order a slight retrenchment. The position was not only extremely tricky for the KOSBs who, I could see, were now out on a limb; reports from other sectors of the perimeter suggested some German impatience at our continued resistance. At 6.40 pm Lonsdale Force was being attacked. At 7.5 pm the Border Regiment was under pressure. At 8.10 pm the Germans struck at the 10th Battalion which now lost the last of its officers as the houses it was holding were set alight and then stormed.

It was the Germans' Bridge technique being repeated.

Down by the river, things were going badly. The northern end of the Heveadorp Ferry, which had been sunk, was now in German hands. On the far side Sosabowski had come up to the river and, finding neither boats nor rafts, had no alternative but to order his Polish troops to take up defensive positions near Driel. Our day's casualties had already been heavy and there was little food and scarcely any water, while everyone was trying to make the scanty ammunition spin out. I walked round some of our positions and then, back in the hotel cellar, I called a divisional conference to order a contraction of the northern face of the perimeter.

It was a chilly, sullen night. Outside lay the bodies of men still unburied and in the cellar treatment room and the corridors were many wounded for whom the water shortage was most serious. Already men had drained hotel and house radiators and central heating systems, and others had taken chances to procure supplies for the wounded. Seeing the wounded in the cellar, my batman Hancock discussed their plight with one of the Dutch patriots who had attached themselves to the HQ, and the two of them set out in the darkness to find a well which the Dutchmen knew existed some two hundred yards away beyond a meadow. With three water-bottles and three kettles, Hancock crawled behind the Dutchman towards the meadow, where a hayrick was ablaze. Remembering the snipers, Hancock lay low until the glare died a bit. Soon afterwards, they reached the well and found the bucket and winding gear in good order. 'Mind the bucket doesn't rattle against the side.' Hancock whispered and had no sooner got the words out when the Dutchman lost his grip on the handle and the bucket clattered down 'like a dozen mess cans', as Hancock later put it. The Dutchman vanished and Hancock dived into a ditch as rifles and automatics opened from almost every direction.

Hancock stayed in the ditch for forty minutes.

Then, cautiously, he returned to the well and filled the three water-bottles and the kettles.

By the time he got back, the job had taken three hours.

In the hotel I was explaining the divisional position and the need to contract so that we would be much less vulnerable to these probing attacks and also to allow us to stop the gaps through which the enemy was infiltrating. I therefore pulled back the KOSBs a few houses, brought over the Recce Squadron with the Independent Company and a squadron of sappers to the eastern side under Hackett, and formed the Divisional RASC into a small force which went into the line between Boy Wilson's men and Lonsdale Force.

Our horseshoe was now roughly 1000 yards wide at the base, broadening to 1200 at the top, by 2000 deep – and already we had lost many of the men we had originally moved into it. I reported to Corps:

No knowledge elements of Div in Arnhem for 24 hours. Balance of Div in very tight perimeter. Heavy mortaring and machine-gun fire followed by local attacks. Main nuisance SP guns. Our casualties heavy. Resources stretched to utmost. Relief within 24 hours vital.

In the cellar of the Hartenstein, the sergeant-major was going round with a mess tin. He had appointed himself guardian of the rations for the duration and was making absolutely sure that there was a fair and equal distribution of whatever was going. When he reached me, he said: 'Two this time, sir.'

I collected my ration of two boiled sweets.

# CHAPTER SIX

As THE cold grey light of the misty dawn broke over Arnhem on Friday, September 22nd, I was awakened with the news that our liaison officer with the Poles, Lieutenant-Colonel Stevens who had dropped with them the day before, had crossed the river and was now waiting to see me. He had no news about XXX Corps' efforts to effect our relief, but he had considerately brought a copy of Thursday morning's *The Times* which he now pressed into my hand with due aplomb. 'You will find there are some references to the operation, sir,' he said. I asked him to tell me what he could about the Poles' situation and meantime thumbed through to the main news page where I read:

## CORRIDOR OF ARMOUR
## THROUGH HOLLAND
### GERMAN COUNTER-ATTACKS ON
### THE FLANKS

Not by what it said, but because it was in my hands, *The Times* lent a momentary and purely artificial security to our position; it represented our first link with the outside world.

Just as the dawn bombardment began, making the ground tremble and the hotel shake and driving some soldiers into the relative calm of the cellars – they were firmly but humanly dispersed to their defence positions by the sergeant-major – I received a signal:

> 43 Div ordered to take all risks to effect relief today and are directed on ferry. If situation warrants you should withdraw to or cross ferry.

I signalled: 'We shall be glad to see you.' By this time, however, we had lost control of the ferry, but I intended to try to re-take it.

Despite this exchange of signals, I was not reassured that XXX Corps were aware of our predicament. It was essential to acquaint Horrocks, and my own corps commander, Browning, of the very desperate nature of events north of the river. The urgency of our situation needed to be driven home, and I now decided to send a senior officer across the river to make everything plain. I sent for Charles Mackenzie who, as chief staff officer, knew as much about the state of affairs as anyone. In view of what was going on south of the river, my scepticism was not misplaced. Mercifully, we were spared any knowledge at this time of the scale of the efforts being made. Horrocks's plan involved the break-out from the Nijmegen bridgehead of Major-General G. I. Thomas's 43rd Division, one brigade of which was to head along the main road through Elst to Arnhem while another brigade swung left through Oosterhout towards the ferry at Hevea-dorp. Horrocks assumed that Thomas would put his troops across the Waal during Thursday night in readiness for a dawn attack. In fact, no move was made until Friday morning and by the time the Somersets moved towards Oosterhout one fortuitous advantage had already been lost. The thick mist was beginning to clear. Under its cover, however, a bold and enterprising troop of the Household Cavalry comprising several armoured-cars dashed through the enfolding greyness, accelerated at high speed through Oosterhout, and joined the Poles near Driel.

Behind them, as the mist cleared, the Somersets were halted at Oosterhout. With them were a troop of 17-pounder guns, a tank squadron, a battery of SP guns – and the advance was held up by a German defence which was later reported as 'a tank and some infantry'.

The battle continued throughout the morning.

And the other prong of the attack had come up against powerful German defences before Elst.

Meantime the Germans were renewing their local attacks around the perimeter. Their snipers were more numerous inside our lines, and the ambitious character with his sights on the rear door of Divisional HQ was again provoking strong language among those whose dignity he ruffled. I was standing close to this door inside the hotel hall talking to Iain Murray when bullets from this familiar foe started pinging into the walls. I had heard earlier reports of his prowess, some of which went so far as to claim that he had put several shots in one door and out of the other. A patrol organized by Laurie Hardman who, as an administrative staff officer, now had no job, set out to put paid to the sniper. Hardman's anti-sniper section were proving successful, and I hoped that they would be able to remove this particular German.

At times, the German mortaring seemed heavier than ever so that it was impossible to make oneself heard above the din. And now my attention was drawn to a strange missile which had landed in front of the hotel without exploding; it was a solid cylinder with a pointed end and a handle attachment, the like of which I had never seen before.

Mackenzie arrived now, and I told him that I wanted him to go over to Browning and Horrocks and make our situation unmistakably known and also to find out all he could about the efforts and whereabouts of the relief force. 'It's necessary that they should know that the division no longer exists as such and that we are now merely a collection of individuals holding on.' Mackenzie, a slightly built Scot with an air about him of immense responsibility, covered up whatever mis-givings he may have harboured about such a hair-raising mission. 'Make clear to them, Charles,' I added, 'that we're terribly short of men, ammunition, food and medical supplies, and that we need some DUKWs to ferry the Poles across. If supplies don't arrive tonight it may be too late.' The ferrying arrangements would soon need priority, and their specialist nature suggested that it would be useful also to send Eddie Myers, a most able engineer, with Mackenzie.

As they left, I asked them also to try and have a look at the river banks in order to give the advancing elements of the 43rd Division some reliable picture of crossing possibilities. I wished them luck and called: 'Above all, do try and make them realize over there what a fix we're in.'

Mackenzie and Myers made their way down towards the river near Oosterbeek Church, and moved stealthily to the spot where Myers had hidden an inflatable dinghy – one of the very few still left unpunctured. For some distance they floated the dinghy along a ditch parallel with the river. Suddenly, they found themselves being escorted by a sturdy sergeant-major armed with a Bren. They turned left, crouching as they followed a hedge leading to the river. The mist had cleared now, but there was a certain amount of haze when they got to the water's edge. The river looked formidably wide and they quickly discussed which of them should row, and the job fell to Mackenzie. Beyond the flood bank on the south side, the ground was disconcertingly open and flat. Several bursts of machine-gun fire had already been aimed at them and had been off target. Now they strained their eyes for a glimpse of the Poles who by arrangement should welcome them. They discerned two steel helmets which could have belonged to Poles or to Germans. For two or three minutes they lay low in a trench, and then Mackenzie stepped out clutching a white handkerchief in case of emergency while Myers stayed put – in case the men were Germans.

All was well. One of the soldiers was a Pole, the other a British liaison officer. They had brought bicycles for the two emissaries, and together the four men rode off through the river haze towards the Poles, who were engaged in beating off some fierce German attacks from the direction of Elst. It was also clear that the Poles had been losing, and were still losing, men to the German guns sited on the commanding promontory north of the river from which the Border Regiment had been pushed the day before. Amid all this hectic activity, Major-General Sosabowski was making inspirational tours of his brigade on a bicycle.

By giving the Germans so much trouble in the Driel area, the Poles were indirectly assisting the 43rd Division in its attempts to break through. Mackenzie lost no time now that he was with the Poles and the troop of Household Cavalry in signalling Horrocks with information about the Division's extreme condition. Horrocks replied: 'Everything will be done to get the essentials through.'

However good were Horrocks's intentions, the fact yet remains that the progress of XXX Corps in our direction was discouragingly slow. Oosterhout was not cleared until about 5 pm this Friday by an attack supported by more than a hundred guns. It was close country with many orchards. The battle is said to have yielded only 139 German prisoners, one obsolete tank, five flak guns and an 88-mm gun. And the casualties of the battalion of the 43rd Division involved in this action totalled nineteen wounded. Within the perimeter men were being killed and hundreds of soldiers were being wounded a second time as they lay in nine overcrowded buildings used by the medical services. Some of the wounded were killed on their stretchers as the German mortars blasted the area. And the Germans themselves had coined their own name for our tiny perimeter.

They were calling it The Cauldron.

Thus we remained alone, unaware of the disappointing events on the south side of the river. We were still concerned to keep open this vital bridgehead through which Monty could come with his drive into Germany.

It was costing the 1st Airborne Division dearly.

The Germans were now making increasing use of their SP guns, which were setting fire to houses in our defence line. Lonsdale Force reported that they had destroyed another one. The Independent Company got another. Flames crackled in the drizzling rain as men stalked the SP guns and took on the following German infantry. Around Oosterbeek Church they were mixing it with Tiger tanks and an SP which persistently ventured round a corner and fired into positions occupied by a mixed force under a 3rd Battalion major called Allan Bush, assisted by my young acquaintance of the early siege in the town, Jimmy Cleminson. They were backed up by a lean and astonishing colour-sergeant who rejoiced under the name of Callaghan and who proceeded to raise the men's morale with a nice line of blarney; at critical moments he was seen wandering among the wounded wearing a dusty Dutch top hat, very tall by British standards, and saying: 'It doesn't matter at all. Nothin' could hit me under this.'

Near by was Robert Cain's section and a Polish anti-tank gun crew. In order to be quick off the mark in retaliation the Poles kept their gun in an exposed place. When a Tiger appeared the Poles dashed to their gun, fired, and then, hit or miss, win or die, charged down the road straight into the shocked Germans. Their bravery was costly and soon Cleminson's batman was among the replacements serving the anti-tank gun. When the SP rumbled round the corner of the street once more, neither the Poles' gun nor Cain's Piat could be brought to bear directly; so Cain took it on by lobbing Piat bombs over the house. It was an almost vertical shot, and during the process a shell from the SP in retaliation brought down the house chimney pot and at the same time killed a gunner officer, Ian Meikle, who was directing Cain's fire. There was plenty of visual evidence of Cain's very active opposition on this day and that following.

Not far away from the scene of all this activity, in the white-fronted house next to Oosterbeek Church, the wounded now were crammed in bloody profusion in every room, on the stairs and even in the stokehole. Men lay under tables and even in the open-hearthed fireplace. It had been a terrible day. At one stage, the battle was so fierce that some shaken soldiers came into the house and discussed in awed tones the accuracy of the German snipers. 'They shoot you in the back,' one of them said. They were surprised when Mrs Ter Horst intervened to calm them and restore their spirits. 'Each of you is a better shot than those snipers,' she announced reassuringly. 'Any one of you can beat them.' The brave Dutchwoman was an inspiration to the orderlies and the wounded, some of whom were making a regular suicide run to a water pump in a neighbouring garden sixty yards away across a stretch of ground strewn with British dead. Another bucket of water was brought and both the bombardier and Mrs Ter Horst noticed that the water was red. They knew each other's thoughts. 'I can't send for any more,' the bombardier said, looking out across the suicide run. 'I'd never forgive myself.' He dropped some disinfectant into the water and went off to boil it. Later it was discovered that the dye from a parachute on a house roof had been rainwashed into the bucket. Despite their original intentions, the medical staff had been compelled now to take advantage of Mrs Ter Horst's offer to make use of her larder: they took fruit preserves first, then

146

beans and carrots but left a piece of meat despite her exhortations that they must have it.

Under the window of the sun-room lay a captain named Frank King. He had just been showing Mrs Ter Horst some photographs of his sister's children and now he heard Morph Martin, the young doctor, asking a soldier less badly wounded than the rest to make room for a serious case. From where he lay on raised trestles with leg wounds from a grenade burst and a bullet hole through his chest, King saw the fear on the soldier's face as he now left the security of the Red Cross. Not long after this, a shell demolished a section of wall by the window where King had been. Mrs Ter Horst dared not ask about his fate, but there were men who said they had seen him going out before the explosion. King had been so moved by the displaced soldier's plight that he had rolled off his stretcher and climbed through the window, taking a dead man's rifle – a German weapon. He stumbled towards the church and then into a cellar. His action undoubtedly saved his life.

There were strong draughts in the windowless house whose doors could not be closed because of the pressure of wounded, yet even those could not dispel the stench of blood and sweat and filth and the sickly sweet smell of death. And as the night approached those in the house were made all too well aware of the activity which now blew up inside the perimeter and across the river where a mobile force of British tanks, Bren carriers and DUKWs had reached the Poles after covering ten miles in exactly one hour.

This move had followed an order from Horrocks, who on learning of the ineffectiveness of the two thrusts by the 43rd Division had ordered General Thomas to concentrate on clearing Oosterhout. The strong mobile column would then follow through. When the first tank of this column came up with the Poles, it was blown up by a Polish mine. The troop commander was understandably annoyed and said to Sosabowski, 'For God's sake see that the rest of my tanks get through.' A moment later, a second tank came to grief and for an uncomfortably long moment Mackenzie saw himself in the role of peacemaker among allies.

With Sosabowski and the commander of the DCLI, Lieutenant-Colonel George Taylor, who was all for striking along towards the main bridge, Mackenzie worked out a plan to get the Poles across the river. In the darkness, two companies of the DCLI moved into positions covering the intended crossing places. Two DUKWs headed towards the river, only to become bogged in a deep ditch, and it was found that the river banks were too steep and slushy to permit launchings. Downriver, Eddie Myers was trying to arrange boats and improvised rafts. As this work went on, Mackenzie sent a message to Boy Browning saying that he would try to reach Corps HQ next morning.

In view of the efforts now being made south of the river the time had come to order the remnants of the Border Regiment to have another crack at re-taking the dominating promontory of Westerbouwing. I gave out this order, and now dictated my situation report:

> Perimeter unchanged. Positions heavily shelled and mortared during day. Minor attacks defeated. Some SP guns knocked out. Assistance given by supporting artillery forward Div. Intend ferry some Poles over tonight. Small attack direction ferry first light tomorrow. Morale high.

Everyone had now settled down to the business of keeping the Germans out. Typical of the spirit of the division was the Independent Company. Under Wilson, they had in the new position into which I had moved them continued their task of spreading alarm among the Wehrmacht. They stalked Germans with ruthless dedication. At sniping they were even more formidable than the enemy. Concealed in positions around the Hotel Schoonhord, the dressing station which the enemy had taken, they now proceeded to pick off the German sentries. In a raid, some of Wilson's men kidnapped three Germans from behind their own lines and soon afterwards a voice came up on the radio telephone saying, 'You must let our boys go. Otherwise we'll come and take your Sunray' (Sunray was my callsign).

Wilson chuckled into the microphone: 'Come and get him if you can.'

In order, as he put it, to 'cheer them up at Division' Wilson had taken to calling on me late at night with amusing stories of his men's adventures and duels, physical and verbal, with the Germans. On this night he took a few moments off to tell me that his company was very happy up there. 'We cooked a goat today and we have enough water for brewing up for some nights to come.' It seemed that when they moved to their new position on the north-east side they had taken over a house belonging to a far-sighted doctor who had taken the precaution of filling his bath before the Germans cut the water supplies. 'My God, I only just managed to save it, though. I found two chaps just about to use it for their ablutions.'

Down by the river, the Poles were still making eager efforts to cross. Shortly before midnight some thirty-five of them succeeded after being swept by the strong current some distance from the points where guides were posted. They made a landfall not far from Oosterbeek Church. Pip Hicks took them under command. Meanwhile, I was awakened and told that Major Breeze, commander of the force of the Border Regiment detailed to make the attack on Westerbouwing, was waiting to see me. He was quite plainly concerned about the likely outcome. 'The men are pretty exhausted,' he reported, 'and even if we're able to establish ourselves on the high ground we will very likely be pushed off again quickly for lack of men in support.' I agreed that a failure at this stage would be fatal, and that instead of risking a withdrawal after a brief occupation of the height they should stay in their present positions.

The Poles were still trying to put men across the river. Many were drowned in the fast-flowing waters, and some were swept down into the hands of the enemy.

In spite of the most resolute bids – one sapper officer, David Storrs, rowed his two-man rubber boat twenty-three times across the river – no more than fifty Poles had reached the perimeter by first light.

The dawn of Saturday, September 23rd, was grey and damp and a clammy mist hung over the battlefield. It was drizzling

DISPOSITIONS AT 23·59 hrs – 22 Sep 1944

Johanna Hoeve

Lichtenbeek

7 KOSB

GP

9 Fd Coy

156 PARA

21 PARA Coy

IO PARA

4 Bde HQ PL

GP

1 BORDER Coy

GP

LONSDALE FORCE

RA

Oosterbeek

Heveadorp

Ferry

Neder Rhine

0    ½    1 mile

with rain from a heavy, forbidding sky as the morning 'hate' opened on schedule and there was the usual gravitation of men to the cellars. The wetness of it all and the congestion added to the normal strains and discomforts of battle and tempers were easily ruffled. The senior administrative officer, Lieutenant-Colonel Henry Preston, started to shave at the ops table and was promptly berated for such sacrilege and forced to make a hurried exit. I do not suppose there was ever such a mixed force in such a small area during any battle, and in these conditions the sergeant-major excelled himself. More than anyone, he maintained order throughout the cellars and the environs of the hotel and he was prompt to allocate the stragglers who appeared from time to time to slit trenches and other defence places. Unlike the more traditional type of Guards NCO, he hardly raised his voice and his insistent dignity caused everyone to heed his instructions without a murmur. One of the more obvious factors at this time of crisis was the high value of the superbly trained ex-Guards warrant officers and NCOs whom Boy Browning had initially taken into the division.

All the way round the perimeter, we were now familiar with the enemy's tactics of prodding with small parties of infantry backed up by SPs, tanks and flame-throwers. The glider pilots especially came in for some heavy treatment now as SPs blasted them out of their houses east of the Hartenstein. Hackett called for artillery support ahead of them, and the 64th Medium laid on another shoot that was as impressive in its accuracy as in its power. But the SPs came on again, driving the glider pilots out of blazing houses to continue the fight in the once-neat suburban gardens. This brought the fighting all too close to Divisional HQ, and I was troubled by the thought that the Germans might burst along the south road and cut off the division from the river. They would have to smash the Lonsdale Force, which was fighting strongly in the south-east corner of the perimeter along the rising ground on the Arnhem side of the church. At 9.45 am I reported:

Spasmodic shelling and mortaring during night. Otherwise little change in perimeter. Several attacks by infantry and SP guns or tanks supported by extremely heavy mortaring and shelling are in progress on north-east corner of perimeter. 50 Poles ferried across river during night. Leading infantry 43 Div have arrived south bank. Hope they will be able to cross under mist. Sup situation serious. Majority no rations last 24 hours. Amn short – latter may be accompanying party from south.

On the south bank, Mackenzie and Myers prepared for the next stage of their task. At first light, Mackenzie asked the tank troop commander for a lift back towards Nijmegen and Browning's HQ. He was told that this would be too difficult without escort. The leader of the Household Cavalry's armoured-car troop which had dashed through the mist the previous morning intervened and said, 'What we did yesterday we should be able to do today in the reverse direction. The mist is better today.'

And so the party set out – a dingo scout car with the section commander in the lead, an armoured-car carrying Mackenzie, a second armoured-car with Myers, and another dingo at the rear.

Soon they came upon a German tank immobilized by the DCLI the night before and now blocking a crossroads. The leading dingo went ahead to test the clearance – there were deep ditches on either side – and at that moment a German half-track appeared from behind a church less than a hundred yards away.

The dingo kept going, very fast, and got clear.

Mackenzie's armoured-car fired on the German vehicle which hit back and then moved behind a tree. The armoured-car driver reversed to bring it in sight again but in doing so put the vehicle into the ditch. It toppled over, with its gun beneath it. Myers's armoured-car and the other dingo disappeared to call up support.

With one Sten gun between them, Mackenzie and the crew of two from the armoured-car took cover in a ditch separating an orchard from a turnip field and then hid under a stack of prunings. They could hear their pursuers stalking among the turnips and calling on them to surrender. One German approached within ten yards. 'Any nearer, and you must shoot,' Mackenzie told the Life Guardsman with the Sten. 'Then we'll bolt for it.' But the German turned away. After a while, the three men heard the armoured-car returning and the clatter of accompanying tanks. As Myers's armoured-car and the other dingo drove on towards Nijmegen the tanks opened fire on the church and Mackenzie and his two companions emerged from the ditch waving their caps. They were greeted with a salvo from the British, but luckily for them the aim was poor. They were recognized before the sights were readjusted.

Saturated and shivering with cold, Mackenzie resumed his journey. He reached Corps HQ some time after Myers, and both officers according to Browning were 'putty coloured like men who had come through a Somme winter'. Despite the hardships of their journey, and its importance, it achieved little. Mackenzie especially was discouraged by the reactions his news produced both at Browning's HQ and at XXX Corps. It is clear now that other problems were pressing on Browning, for early in the afternoon German tanks and infantry cut the 2nd Army corridor between Veghel and Uden. Horrocks had to send back a Guards brigade to help the Americans restore the line of communication. This diversion was bound to weaken the drive towards Arnhem.

Nonetheless, Mackenzie had misgivings that he had convinced nobody about the seriousness of our plight. He felt there was a lack of urgency at XXX Corps. His scepticism mounted when General Thomas ordered the commander of the leading brigade of his 43rd Division to take the Polish Brigade under command and to attempt a crossing into the perimeter at night. Compared with the other snags Mackenzie could foresee, the renowned independence of Sosabowski was only a minor obstacle. This plan was not going to produce a crossing of sufficient strength to be of any real use. As he made his way back towards the Neder Rhine with the leading brigade of the 43rd Division he pondered on the grim inevitability of it all. When they came upon the Poles, he called on Sosabowski to smooth the way for the new command arrangement. It was thoroughly unsatisfactory and showed little regard for the fact that the Poles were a brigade group of great fighting potential under an experienced commander holding the rank of Major-General. To have put him under a comparatively junior brigadier was just inviting friction. In any case, Mackenzie knew that this combined force was not nearly strong enough to keep us going north of the river.

In The Cauldron there were times when it seemed no living thing could survive above ground. The shelling and mortaring were kept up with a fury designed to bend the will of the little force now remaining. And along the fringe of the perimeter the Germans were attacking vigorously, especially against Lonsdale Force in the south-east and also to the north and north-east where it was seen that many more tanks were in operation. The tactics were the same – to drive the British out of the houses either by demolishing them with high explosives or burning them with incendiary shells. 'Houses are a snare unless we can keep the SPs round the corner,' Hackett remarked. As those still resisting went to ground, the wounded in the dressing stations and other buildings were enduring unspeakable conditions of hardship. By now the Taffelberg Hotel had been hit twice by shellfire and some of the wounded were showered with rusty water from the pipes.

Movement about the perimeter was difficult not only because of the amount of splinters flying about but also because of the snipers, more of whom had infiltrated. There were physical obstacles, too. Roads and lanes were blocked with shattered masonry, fallen trees and abandoned vehicles. The few jeeps that were left had only a limited usefulness, mainly to the medical officers. On the faces of the men I could see the cumulative wear of lack of sleep and food, and exposure. Dirt-caked and with heavy-lidded, reddened eyes, they had not an unlimited endurance before them; but their spirit was magnificent to see.

Towards midday, Hackett was summoned from his HQ not far from the Hartenstein to meet a German officer who had appeared in a half-track under the white flag. The German saluted and without preliminaries announced with exaggerated formality: 'We are about to deliver an attack on this side of the perimeter. I intend to put down a mortar and artillery concentration on your forward positions.' Turning towards the road, he pointed to our casualty clearing station. 'We know that you have wounded there and we do not wish to put down a barrage that will hit them.' Hackett wondered what the fellow was leading up to, and was not surprised when the German said, 'I am asking you to move your forward positions six hundred yards farther back.'

As Hackett was quick to see, the request was impossible to meet: if the line had been moved back by the distance demanded by the German, it would leave Divisional HQ some two hundred yards behind the German lines. We had a laugh over this when Hackett came to see me. Playing for time, he had told the German: 'I must talk it over with my commander first.' Reluctantly, the German concurred and they agreed to meet again at 3 pm.

'You will have to do as you think best,' I told Hackett. 'I am not going to influence you.'

'I'm afraid that the casualty clearing station will have to take its chance,' he replied.

'That is the conclusion I would have come to,' I said.

Promptly at 3 pm Hackett and the German met again on the road close to Hackett's HQ. 'With great regret,' said Hackett in his competent German, 'we cannot agree to any move.'

The casualty station consisted of buildings on both sides of the main road which ran right through the perimeter. It was therefore in an obvious target area for any bombardment the Germans might make preparatory to a thrust into the heart of the perimeter.

We watched for the first barrage, and soon it came, but farther south.

This time the casualty station was spared.

Wherever I went the question was the same: 'What has happened to the 2nd Army?' My answers had to be necessarily evasive for I would have given much myself to know what was going on south of the river. I was also baffled by the lack of fighter support. In view of the complete superiority of the Allied air forces in western Europe, it was disappointing to find ourselves so starved of offensive air support. A flight of Spitfires had appeared during the day and pulled out of a power dive on one of our own medical establishments only just in time, and a few sorties had been flown around the perimeter edge by rocket-firing Typhoons. At four o'clock in the afternoon came the usual gallant attempts by the re-supply crews to get stuff in to us. Although we did not know it, this was the last attempt of its kind from England. Air Vice-Marshal Leslie Hollinghurst, who was controlling these operations from Eastcote, near Ruislip, had naturally been concerned about the high cost to his squadrons. On the 19th, thirteen of the aircraft which tried to re-supply us were lost and ninety-seven damaged; on the 20th, nine and sixty-two, while on the 21st, seven out of ten aircraft belonging to 190 Squadron were lost. And now, on this Saturday after-noon, the flak was taking further heavy toll. Out of 123 aircraft, sixty-three were damaged and six lost. Earlier in the week, the extent of the losses and the uncertainty about the usefulness of the dropping points had prompted Air Commo-dore Darvall, commanding one of the supply groups, to inspect at first hand the tactical situation as it affected re-supply. The upshot of this visit was that one of the supply squadrons was moved from England to an airfield near Brussels on this Saturday. Darvall also suggested to Horrocks, Browning and Air Vice-Marshal Broadhurst, commanding 83 Group of the 2nd Tactical Air Force, that fighters might be used for supply dropping in place of the more vulnerable Dakotas and Stirlings. It appears that there was some measure of unanimity about the advisability of such a move, but the fact remains that no fighters joined in re-supply missions over Arnhem.

On this Saturday afternoon only a minute proportion of the panniers came our way, and the food contents were taken to the wounded.

The attacks all round the perimeter continued. Near the main dressing station Boy Wilson's private war both with weapons and propaganda was reaching another climax. Upset by the Independent Company's proficiency at picking off German guards, the Germans now brought up a self-propelled gun and then tuned-in to Wilson by wireless with an ultimatum. 'Withdraw your men or we will blast the dressing station to bits.'

Wilson chose to bluff it out. 'We have a lot of Piats here,' he replied. 'If you don't clear off we'll blast you out.'

He won a verbal victory. The gun withdrew, though the Germans later renewed their complaints about his behaviour and their threats to blow down the dressing station.

I prepared a signal in which I wanted to reiterate the extremity of our situation and to make it clear that there was little profit in our staying unless XXX Corps could come up pretty quickly. Nevertheless, I didn't want to give any impression that we were all for hooking it. I read through the draft twice and when Hackett, Hicks and Loder-Symonds called during the evening I showed them the signal and asked for their views. They allayed my fears that I might have overdone it, and at 8.15 pm it was dispatched:

Many attacks during day by small parties inf, SP guns and tanks including flamethrowers. Each attack accompanied by very heavy mortaring and shelling within Div perimeter. After many alarms and excursions the latter remains substantially unchanged. Although very thinly held. Physical contact not yet made with those on south bank of river. Resup a flop, small quantities amn only gathered in. Still no food and all ranks extremely dirty owing to shortage of water. Morale still adequate, but continued heavy mortaring and shelling is having obvious effects. We shall hold but at the same time hope for a brighter 24 hours ahead.

The rain had ceased, and it was a clear starlit night. Around us, the encircling Germans were very active. They were obviously aware that a further effort would be made during the night to reinforce us, and put in some fierce attacks. The KOSBs had to pull in a bit, and the Recce Squadron was blasted from its houses and was forced to give a hundred yards. There was also a withdrawal by the remains of the 10th Battalion. However, the horseshoe was intact except for the infiltrating snipers, and the pulling-in made little difference. Not far away Bomber Command was busy and the fires and flares of this attack cast a lurid shadowy glare over the horizon. The gasworks in the south-west corner of the perimeter was blazing and casting reflections on the contested river.

On the far bank, Charles Mackenzie took cover until the glare and the fury subsided. When he reached the water's edge with his dinghy a boat loomed out of the shadows and Mackenzie changed places with a gentleman of the RAF who after being shot down had reached the perimeter and was now on his way back to base. The sapper officer running the ferry accepted his strange role with an air of nonchalance. As they started back, Mackenzie was aware of other craft around them on the swirling river. In fact, Myers wasn't far away: he was preoccupied with the launching of the 130th Brigade's assault boats carrying more Poles across. Mackenzie was delivered alongside one of the groynes, which spaced the entire length of the river, into the hands of a guide who then led him across the open low-lying ground towards Ooster-beek and the Hartenstein Hotel.

They crossed the road not far from the house near Ooster-beek Church where Mrs Ter Horst was just finishing a reading of Psalm 91 to the children and neighbours who shared the cellar. She blew out the candle and climbed the crowded steps past wounded men. Earlier, when the shelling and mortaring had reached a new crescendo and it seemed that the house could not possibly stay intact, there was talk among the Dutch civilians in the cellar of moving out under the protection of a white flag. The British officers in the house considered the risk was too great. And by now Kate Ter Horst had made her own decision: constantly torn between her children and the badly wounded soldiers upstairs she knew now that she could not possibly leave 'the defenceless ones' as she called the wounded troops. Now, she emerged from the cellar and sought out the padre who was busy about the place and told him of her Psalm reading. 'I have no time to read to the boys,' he told her wearily. He handed her his English Bible. She went through the house now, reading by the light of a pocket-lamp shaded by an orderly's hands to all who wanted to listen. The wounded lay so close together that she had to be careful where she placed her feet. There were moments when the quiet soothing voice of the Dutch-woman was the only sound in a room filled with men. The meaning of words which once would have meant little was now clear to them: 'Thou shalt not be afraid for the terror by night; nor for the arrow that flieth by day.'

Outside the house lay many dead.

Near by, Lonsdale Force and the gunners prepared for another troubled night.

At the Hartenstein I talked to Loder-Symonds and Wilson and agreed to let Hackett have the first body of Poles to come across. Mackenzie returned just before midnight. I offered him my chair by the wine-rack and he started to tell me about the 43rd Division's plan in concert with the Poles. He was torn between telling me what Horrocks and Thomas thought was going to happen, and the contrary view he held as a result of what he had seen and heard. He was certain in his own mind now that no reinforcement of any consequence could possibly arrive in time, but he chose to gloss over this inter-pretation and to give me the official picture which was rosier. It was not until years afterwards that I learned of Mackenzie's dilemma.

At the riverside, the Poles found that the 43rd Division's leading brigade had only twelve boats. By the early hours of Sunday, September 24th, no more than two hundred Polish officers and men had reached us. Some were killed even before they could be put into position under Hackett.


What remained of the Division still held roughly to the perimeter we had established, though here and there we had given up a hundred yards. We had now been in Arnhem and Oosterbeek for almost a week; so much had happened that it now required an effort of the imagination to recall the landings. The water scarcity was a severe handicap and the young soldiers especially were feeling the effects of hunger. As an older man I was possibly less affected than they were, and I remembered a theory that occasional fasting has the effect of making one more clear-headed. Nevertheless I felt some sympathy for the hungry, especially after hearing of one ration distribution the night before – 'one sardine and some biscuits per man'. Even the men awarded that diet fared better than some in other sectors of the line.

Despite the mortaring and the general discomfort of those still combatant – the stench which now pervaded the area was sickening – it was the wounded who were suffering most. Even the war correspondents did all they could to help. From the bottom of a slit trench writing was not easy. Later Stanley Maxted, of the BBC, and Alan Wood, a newspaperman, produced excellent reports on the battle.

Hackett, on the way back to his command post after arranging for the arrival of the Poles, was caught by a mortar burst and hit in the thigh and stomach. A Recce Squadron man accompanying him was also hit. When Hackett found that the man's leg was broken and that his own was only bleeding he made his way to the Hartenstein and collected two stretcher-bearers. He led them to the place where the man lay, and then sought attention for himself.

At about this time Graeme Warrack was finding his job as chief doctor the busiest he had ever known. He came to Divisional HQ to give me the medical picture, and twice had to take cover. Then he went off to see Hackett. For as long as Hackett could remember he had been trying to persuade Warrack to open the brandy which he knew doctors carried; yet even on such occasions as St Andrew's night and on the ship coming home from Italy Warrack had made unsatisfactory excuses.

Now Hackett saw his chance. 'You can now produce those medical comforts,' he called to Warrack.

Warrack looked sorry. 'The brandy has run out,' he explained.

'And this,' retorted Hackett, 'is the moment we've waited eighteen months for!'

Warrack gave him a shot of morphia.

What he now saw at Divisional HQ, where the wounded lay congested in the cellars, added to Warrack's conviction that something would have to be done soon to get the patients settled. They were not getting enough attention and in some of the medical buildings they were being badly knocked about. Surgery was almost impossible, supplies of morphia and bandages were low, and the wounded were not getting the fluids or the warmth they needed. Many were lying on stone floors with one blanket between two men. I knew Warrack well enough to know that he was not overstating the case; usually so genial and bouncy, even under duress, he was now deeply upset about the entire medical situation.

'Well, what's on your mind, Graeme?'

'If you don't mind,' he said, 'I'd like to go and see the German commander and arrange for the evacuation of our wounded to his hospitals in Arnhem.'

I did not want to encourage the Germans to think that we were ready to throw in our hand, yet it would be inhuman to deny the wounded their only chance of recovery. 'All right,' I told Warrack. 'You may make the attempt on condition that the Germans understand that you are a doctor representing your patients and not an official emissary from the division.'

He set off to collect the two people who were to accompany him – Lieutenant-Commander Wolters and a Dutch doctor who was working at the Taffelberg.

I told Iain Murray, who commanded one of the glider pilot wings, to take over Hackett's responsibilities for the eastern side of the perimeter. I was increasingly concerned about the lack of news from the other side of the river, and the further delays in the organization of the crossing, and I told signals to try to raise General Thomas on the radio link. While this was being done, I went over to look at Hackett who was grey-faced and in some sort of coma. I felt sure he would die. A few minutes later I was called to the radio and heard Thomas's voice. I tried to convey to him the critical state in which the Division now found itself. 'We are being very heavily shelled and mortared *now* from areas very close to our positions,' I explained.

To my intense annoyance, Thomas replied with some impatience: 'Well, why don't you counter-mortar them? Or shell them?'

Imagining the cosier environment from which he was speaking, I flared up. 'How the hell can we?' I retorted. 'We're in holes in the ground. We can't see more than a few yards. And we haven't the ammunition.' I found his gratuitous advice infuriating. This was just like Thomas, who sometimes could make me very angry. Having worked with him before, however, I knew that he would do what he could to help us. I suppose I was getting on edge and touchy. I was also sure that he had not got the situation clear at all.

At this time I called for offensive air support and Typhoons rocketed German positions; but there were not many of them, and the volume of fire from the enemy mortars was not noticeably affected. I wondered then why so few fighters came to our aid. It was not until after the operation that certain disturbing facts came to light. By far the most serious was a decision to keep the 2nd Tactical Air Force out of the battle zone during airborne and re-supply missions. The Americans insisted on this restriction in order to avoid any mix-up with the re-supply force, and while there were times when the 2nd Tactical Air Force was prevented by bad weather from interfering on our behalf there were undoubtedly occasions when there was little to stop them except a plan which nobody seemed prepared to modify in the critical phase of the battle. Further, there was a tendency for the RAF not to accept targets which could not be specifically pinpointed; though this was a difficulty encountered by Browning and not by me.

The air control of the battle was also too remote and ought to have been the business of the 2nd Tactical Air Force. A surprising corollary to the weakness of the air plan was that Hollinghurst's HQ at Eastcote had no direct signal link with the 2nd Tactical Air Force on the Continent. When Hollinghurst had announced that the re-supply from England could not continue because of the heavy losses, my representative on the air side at Brereton's HQ, an able staff officer called Bill Campbell, passed on the news to an American colleague. It was Sunday morning, and we had been at Arnhem a week. In his office at Ascot, Brereton's chief of operations, Ralph Stearley, a downright and vigorous American brigadier, heard Campbell with some incredulity. 'Goddammit!' he bristled. 'We'll dive-bomb the stuff to them with fighter-bombers.' He picked up a telephone and contacted the US Eighth Air Force. 'Can you load up supplies for Arnhem?' he demanded.

The answer was 'Yes'.

Later Stearley informed Campbell that the fighter-bombers'

belly tanks were being loaded with rations and small-arms ammunition. The squadrons would be ready to take off at noon but they must have clearance from the 2nd Tactical Air Force.

By midday no reply had been received. The communications set-up was not geared to cope with such a development, and by the time an answer came it was much too late.

In the perimeter the troops of my division somehow kept going on hidden reserves of energy; but I had no doubt of the exhaustion and strain they were feeling. I was growing sceptical of effective relief, especially after my sharp exchange of words with Thomas. I wondered what had happened to the 52nd Lowland Division which had been held in reserve in England. Under the original plan it was due to be flown in later to Deelen airfield. Perhaps it was being brought over to strengthen the drive. In fact, Browning already had elements of the 52nd holding his own left flank, and Brereton offered to fly the rest of the division into Grave airfield. But on the grounds that there was no room for another division on 'the island' between ourselves and Nijmegen, Monty personally vetoed the scheme.

Meantime, our chief doctor had set about his mission to the Germans. With Wolters and the Dutch doctor he approached the German medical officer in charge at the Hotel Schoon-hord. 'I want to make arrangements for the evacuation of our wounded,' Warrack explained. 'I would like to see your divisional doctor.' The German, a young-looking doctor whose name was Skalka, was at pains to point out that he was the senior German medical officer.

Warrack then asked to be taken to the German commander.

Apparently pleased about the purpose of the mission, Skalka ushered Warrack and Wolters into a jeep flying the Red Cross. Warrack was surprised that he was not blindfolded as they drove along the main road into Arnhem past the wreckage that suggested some violent tornado. The road was strewn with corpses, smashed vehicles, burned-out tanks and jeeps, masonry from the battered houses, and trailing tram-wires. The St Elizabeth Hospital looked fairly intact. Soon, in the heart of the town, they stopped outside the German

HQ and were shown into a room full of strikingly young staff officers. The German chief of staff appeared, a tall, handsome man wearing an Iron Cross. He produced a map on which Warrack pointed out the dressing stations. The German commander now came into the room. He was affable and had plainly been briefed by Skalka about the purpose of the visit. 'I am extremely sorry that there should be this fight between our two countries,' he said.

He would help with the wounded.

Skalka telephoned for all the ambulances that were available to start evacuating the wounded from the 'Kessel' as he kept calling our perimeter.

The Germans were quite obviously impressed by the division's performance in The Cauldron. Warrack was asked to give the number of casualties and in order to underplay our weakness he said there were six hundred, which was only a proportion of the actual number.

When their GOC had departed the young officers produced a bottle of brandy. Warrack refused a drink because, he said, it was too early in the day and he had been fasting and it would therefore probably make him drunk. This remark produced a howl of laugher and, more usefully, a plate of sandwiches which the Germans insisted that Warrack and Wolters should eat. Before he left, Warrack was permitted to help himself to some stocks of morphia captured from us and was also given a bottle of brandy to take away. Then, with Skalka and an armed guard in the jeep, he and Wolters were driven to the St Elizabeth Hospital where the British wounded were faring much better than their comrades who were receiving treatment within the perimeter. They were in proper beds with sheets, and there were Dutch nurses to care for them.

Back in the divisional area, Warrack set going the evacuation arrangements. The Germans had agreed to slacken their fire during the afternoon while the dressing stations and the battlefield were cleared of wounded. Inevitably, there were misunderstandings and difficulties; it is not easy temporarily to still a battle. Hardly had Warrack started the moves when the Taffelberg group of hospital buildings was occupied by the Germans, and the doctors endured some uneasy moments as they cleared combative Germans off the premises. Soon afterwards some 200 walking wounded were cleared from this area. At the other end of the hospital area, the operation was confused because of the number of armed Germans moving in and out of the Red Cross buildings and the fact that the Poles, who had many old scores to settle, saw no legitimate reason for holding their fire. Ultimately a senior doctor, Lieutenant-Colonel Marrable, prevailed upon the Germans to stop and upon the Poles to curb their eagerness until the evacuation was complete. To add to the general uncertainty there were natural qualms as to whether everyone was aware of the evacuation agreement.

Generally, however, this went with surprising efficiency. In addition to the 200 men marched off from the Taffelberg, a further 250 were moved out during this strange afternoon of not quite total war. Among these was Shan Hackett, who was carried with four other wounded, two of them stretcher cases lying across the bonnet, in a jeep. They drove through some shelling on their way to the St Elizabeth Hospital and Hackett was heartened by the evidence he saw all around of the work of the 2nd Army medium guns. He was feeling very sick by the time he was delivered on to the stone floor of the hospital. Near by lay his sergeant clerk, Dudley Pearson, for whom Hackett had an even higher regard after their running fight to get back the divisional area earlier in the battle. Presently a British medical officer, Theo Redman, paused on his rounds and asked Hackett what was wrong with him.

'I've got a hole through the leg and I feel sick,' Hackett replied.

Redman checked him over, observing the serious stomach wound and said, 'When did this happen?'

'Probably the same time I was hit in the leg. I thought a shell cap hit my equipment over the solar plexus. I've been feeling it all day.'

Redman seemed rather worried. 'Where does it come out?' he asked.

'Blimey!' said Hackett. 'Don't ask me!'

Redman made a further inspection and said, 'There's no exit.' His face, Hackett has recalled, fell a yard.

Shortly afterwards, Hackett was given an anaesthetic and he was oblivious of the tour made by an SS doctor in company with one of our divisional surgeons, Lipmann-Kessel. When they reached Hackett, the German had already seen several extreme cases and he was pronouncing a verdict on each. 'That one's no good, and I wouldn't waste time on this.' Of Hackett he remarked, 'We always say – "a head wound or a stomach wound, euthanasia's best".' As casually as he could, Lipmann-Kessel said, 'Oh, I don't know. I think I'll have a go at this one.' Hackett was wearing no badges of rank.

'You're wasting your time,' the German said.

Lipmann-Kessel operated.

Back in The Cauldron, the German shelling and mortaring was causing more casualties to take the places of those fortunate enough to be taken out. It was a terrible, desperate day. In places there was some enemy penetration but the Germans were winkled out by gallant counter-attacks and daring stalks. As evening approached the perimeter was substantially unchanged, but the Germans appeared to be everywhere. In the KOSB area, Payton-Reid's experiences were typical of those of many others in the division. More than once as he inspected his positions, he came across Germans instead of his own men. With Sergeant Tilley, a glider pilot who had appointed himself Payton-Reid's bodyguard, he had just visited one group of men who were rather vague about the location of their neighbours. Payton-Reid and Tilley went round a corner and came on a small building. The sergeant suggested that he should take a look first. He soon came bounding back. 'The trench round there is full of Germans,' he said.

'Did they see you?'

'If they didn't they must be blind.'

'We'd better get out of it,' said Payton-Reid.

They vaulted through the window of a nearby house, but the floor had been blown out and they fell right through to the cellar. Payton-Reid gave the sergeant a leg up so that he could grasp the edge of the hole. Any moment they expected to see the Germans looking down at them. Somehow, Tilley pulled himself clear and then hauled his commander, a stocky, heavily-built officer, to the security of the ground floor. It was not the only place where Payton-Reid found that his men had been pushed out and replaced by Germans. After his adjutant had been wounded in trying to establish the whereabouts of one section, Payton-Reid crawled through furrows of beans and peas across several gardens to find beyond the next row of houses not some of his own troops but a German tank. It was a sitting target. He crawled back and sent away for the only Piat left in the battalion. By the time it arrived, the tank had gone.

On the south side of the river, it was becoming clearer that urgent action was required, and Horrocks, who had visited Driel and talked with Sosabowski, decided that a further attempt to force a crossing should be made on the Monday night, September 25th. Later, when Browning called at his HQ, Horrocks started to expand on his ideas about a crossing west of Arnhem. Browning was now in no doubt about the extremity of our case and soon after his visit to XXX Corps he dictated a letter to me which he sent off by hand. When General Dempsey called at his HQ, Browning repeated Horrocks's plan to get over to us, and said that in his view Horrocks was being somewhat optimistic. 'I think the time has come to withdraw the 1st Division,' he said.

The two commanders immediately went off to see Horrocks, who now outlined his own corps situation and his plan for reinforcing the bridgehead north of the Neder Rhine. He was still very much in favour of getting across. At this stage, however, Model's brilliant generalship not only had us all but trapped in Oosterbeek; he also had XXX Corps out on a precarious limb, and had prevented the two flanking corps – VIII and XII – from making any ground. He had seriously interrupted the single line of communications over which the 2nd Army had to advance, and had upset more than time-tables. Along the airborne carpet the edges were looking distinctly frayed in places. It is likely that Dempsey had such things in mind as he paused for a moment considering

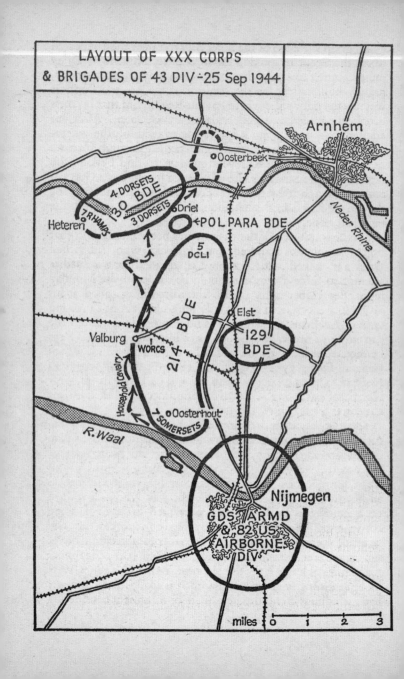

Horrocks's plan. Then he said: 'No. Get them out.' He turned to Browning. 'Is that all right with you?'

Browning assented, and so did Monty, whose approval had to be given. It meant that Monty's plan to roll his armour across the wide plain of north Germany was finished for the time being. He must have known that this decision to bring us out would postpone the end of the war in Europe until the following year. Yet he made his decision promptly.

Meantime, more of the Polish Brigade and the 4th Dorsets were preparing to cross the river, while inside the perimeter the jaded garrison fought on. In some cases it was instinctive resistance; in others, the last instalments of willpower were dredged. There were also the 'bomb-happy' to whom nothing mattered any more. Exhaustion was real. In the broken house that was the KOSB HQ, Payton-Reid called a battalion conference round a table covered in brick dust. There were four men present, including a gunner, Captain Walker, who had become second-in-command, and Sergeant Tilley. Payton-Reid could hear himself talking, distantly. Someone had fallen asleep over the table, and now someone else. Soon all four were slumbering, though not deeply. A little later Payton-Reid came round and awakened the rest.

In the heart of the division – the cellar of the Hartenstein Hotel – the clerk wrote in the official diary: *Never was darkness more eagerly awaited*.

We had lasted one more day.

The Dorsets went into action, crossing the river near the site of the Heveadorp Ferry. The majority were carried by the swift current downstream and landed well beyond the base of our perimeter. They had a sticky passage from the enemy, and suffered a lot of casualties. It was sad that this gallant effort should have so little effect on our situation.

With the Dorsets was Lieutenant-Colonel Tommy Hadden, who had set off with the first lift in command of the Border Regiment. The glider towrope parted while they were still over England. After landing, Hadden managed to get back to an airfield in time to join the second lift the following day. This time, the glider in which he travelled parted from its tug

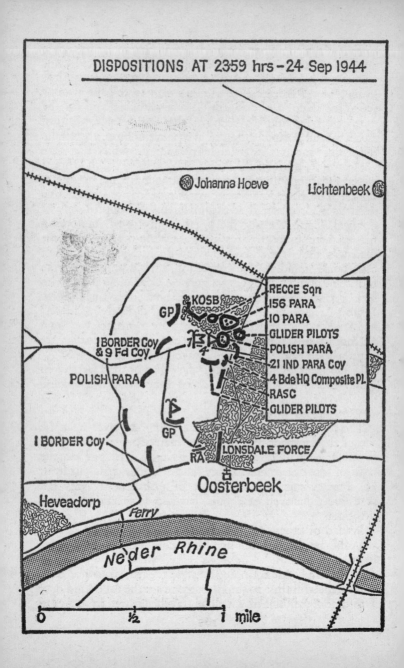

DISPOSITIONS AT 2359 hrs – 24 Sep 1944

Johanna Hoeve

Lichtenbeek

KOSB

GP

RECCE Sqn
156 PARA
10 PARA
GLIDER PILOTS
POLISH PARA
21 IND PARA Coy
4 Bde HQ Composite PL
RASC
GLIDER PILOTS

1 BORDER Coy
& 9 Fd Coy

POLISH PARA

GP

1 BORDER Coy

RA

LONSDALE FORCE

Oosterbeek

Heveadorp

Ferry

Neder Rhine

0        ½        1 mile

over Holland a long way from the landing zone. He had some adventures before he linked up with XXX Corps and came through with the Dorsets. It was a pity that such persistence should be so ill rewarded; for he was soon to become a prisoner.

At the river Eddie Myers was supervising the loading of DUKWs, including one filled with ammunition. He had in his smock pocket the letter from Browning which had been entrusted to Sosabowski during Sunday afternoon. He also carried another letter from General Thomas, the contents of which he had committed to memory. He crossed the river with these documents and headed for the Hartenstein.

Myers had to clamber along the north side of the river, in the lee of the banking, until he was sure he was inside the perimeter. His splashing now and then attracted German attention, but he reached a safe place to come ashore. Looking much the worse for wear, he came into the Hartenstein soon after six o'clock on Monday morning. I opened the letters. Browning had written:

Dear Roy:
Sosabowski will be bringing you this, I hope tonight.
I will not labour your present position, and it may be little consolation to you and the 1st Division when I tell you that the opinion held this side of the river is that the action of the 1st Division has, apart from the killing of the many Boche it has undoubtedly achieved, enabled XXX Corps and the Airborne Corps between them to capture the Nijmegen bridges and to break clean through the main German defence line on the Waal.

From the information at our disposal, the German undoubtedly moved back the bulk of his forces from Nijmegen to Arnhem just before our airborne attack took place, and instead of the Nijmegen crossings being an acutely difficult problem, the Arnhem crossings have become most acute in consequence.

You can rest assured that XXX Corps are doing their maximum under the most appalling difficulties to relieve you. As you know, I am responsible for from inclusive

Nijmegen down the narrow corridor back for approximately 40 miles, and the road has been cut between us and the main body for 24 hours, which does not help matters much. It is now through again, and the Army is pouring to your assistance but, as you will appreciate better than I do, very late in the day.

I naturally feel, not so tired and frustrated as you do, but probably almost worse about the whole thing than you do.

I enclose a copy of a letter from Field Marshal Monty,* and I hope to see you in a day or two.

It may amuse you to know that my front faces in all directions, but I am only in close contact with the enemy for about 8000 yards to the south-east, which is quite enough in present circumstances.

Yours ever,

F. A. M. Browning.

The letter from Thomas, written much later, explained that the 2nd Army plan was not now to form a bridgehead west of Arnhem and that the 43rd Division itself was beginning to feel the effects of German action on 'the island' across from our perimeter. By arrangement between Thomas and myself we were to be withdrawn on a date to be agreed. The withdrawal would be called Operation 'Berlin'. Myers told me about the Dorsets' rough crossing and I went outside thinking that the evacuation would have to be very soon. Already there were the awakening sounds of battle. The wind and the morning dew had not removed the stench and many soldiers still lay unburied on the saturated ground.

There were now about 2500 of us left – a quarter of our original strength. Outnumbered and outgunned for days, men had fought at close quarters and on empty stomachs. The dressing stations were again full.

I could not expect much more of those who were still on their feet. I went back into the hotel, past the men in their slit trenches, and down the steps and along the corridor between the wounded men lying there, some of them with not much longer to live. It was eight o'clock and the German artillery

* In fact, no letter was enclosed.

and mortars were busy again. I ordered the signaller to raise General Thomas. At eight minutes past eight on this morning of Monday, September 25th, he was at the other end.

I said: 'Operation "Berlin" must be tonight.'

# CHAPTER SEVEN

AT THE back of my mind was Gallipoli. As a young officer I had studied this classic withdrawal very thoroughly for a promotion examination. It all came back now: the extreme pains that were taken to thin out the forward positions held at Anzac and in front of the other beaches; the way that the British had contrived to keep up an appearance of opposition until the very last, and the elaborate care with which parties were organized for their move to the beaches. I called Charles Mackenzie over to help me with the evacuation plan. 'You know how they did it at Gallipoli, Charles? Well, we've got to do something like that.' I visualized a pulling-in of the horseshoe line from the northern face and progressing down each flank until it came the turn of those nearest the river. Small parties would be required to raise enough fire to give the impression that we were still about the place. I was also banking on the probability that the Germans, once they were aware of some movement in the perimeter, would assume that it was in the opposite direction; in view of the previous efforts of the Poles to get across, and the foothold the Dorsets had gained, this was a reasonable expectation. We would also have to count on a considerable artillery programme by the XXX Corps gunners, whose performance to date had been beyond praise. There would also be machine-gun fire on the flanks by the 43rd Division from across the river. I hoped that with this protection the deception would be as complete as any of us could expect.

As Mackenzie and I worked out the plan on these lines, Loder-Symonds was dealing with the artillery side. I ordered a divisional conference for 10.30 am. By now, activity around the perimeter was warming up again. There was a scare when some German infantry got into several houses along the road between the Hartenstein Hotel and Hicks's HQ, and ambushed anyone who stirred in the vicinity. It fell to the glider pilots, whose street fighting ability would have done credit to the best-trained infantry, to winkle them out. As a reprisal, the

Germans now brought up three SPs and a Tiger tank. The Tiger moved towards the entrance to Hicks's HQ and stopped by the gate. It was covered by an anti-tank gun but the breech was jammed as a result of mortar fire and another six-pounder had to be brought up. Three rounds were fired and the tank was put out of action. Although there was no more immediate trouble in this area, Pip Hicks was out of breath when he turned up at the Hartenstein having made yet another of those life-or-death sprints across what once had been the Hartenstein's rear lawn. The sniper who had covered this stretch for so long had now been silenced, but a Spandau was raking the area.

Next to appear was Warrack. He gave me the latest casualty situation and told me of his experiences over on the German side. I had already decided that all the doctors would stay behind to look after the wounded. The withdrawal would certainly involve more casualties and a senior officer would be required to organize their collection after the rest had gone.

'I have some important news, Graeme,' I said. 'Tonight we're pulling out. You know what that will mean. You will be needed here with the wounded. I expect all the doctors to remain.'

No man with his mind and legs in good repair can possibly look with equanimity upon capture, but Warrack covered up whatever feelings he experienced at this moment. I had rarely seen this massive, good-natured officer without a smile on his face. He even raised one now.

'What time do you propose to go?' he asked.

I told him we would start crossing at 10 pm.

'I'll try to see you again before then,' he said, and left to begin his own preparations.

In the cellar, I glanced round the tired faces as the conference assembled. Hicks, Iain Murray, Loder-Symonds, Mackenzie and Myers were there.

I said: 'We are to clear out tonight.' I explained that units would withdraw on a time programme by two routes. 'In general those farthest from the river will start first. I don't expect that either of the routes will be free from enemy interference, but they are the best available to us.'

The plan included the posting of guides on both east and

west routes as far as the open marshy land alongside the river. The glider pilots were to be used for this task. In difficult places the routes would be marked with parachute tape. Guides from each unit would make themselves familiar with the routes during the day. Myers's sappers would look after the last stretches to the embarkation points. Men would move in boatload parties of fourteen with their boots muffled and would take evasive action if engaged and only retaliate if it was vital.

On Myers fell the dual responsibility of selecting the routes and fixing the ferry service. He had hardly recovered from his ordeal of crossing the river in both directions only a little time before. Yet he managed to look extremely alert and he was, as usual, full of ideas. There was no need to underline just how vital were his technical experience and his qualities of character to the division's survival. I turned to Robert Loder-Symonds and said that we would expect much from the gunners shooting from 'the island'.

'I'm sure we'll get all we want,' he replied.

Finally I ordered that news of the evacuation should not be broken until it was absolutely necessary to do so. We still had another day's fight ahead and there was always the likelihood of exhausted men falling into German hands and coming under interrogation. Further, when once men start to look over their shoulders their effectiveness is reduced.

Only those who had to know were told now of the plan.

I realized only too well that the cost of pulling out the remnants of my division through a riverside bottleneck already reduced to between 600 and 700 yards might be high – very high.

There was no better way.

Even as the conference was finishing, the gunners down near the church were heavily set upon and sent out an urgent call for infantry and Piats to counter what was a determined German drive to cut us off from the river. There was little we could do to help. One of the batteries was overrun and for a time a sizeable body of Germans was in our perimeter and on a withdrawal route. Told to hold on, the gunners were man-handling their 75-mm pieces and firing over open sights at ranges down to fifty yards. And by such fantastic gunnery they were more than holding their own! As this battle gained momentum, the occupants of Mrs Ter Horst's house, which was right in the middle of it all, expected the Germans to walk in at any moment.

The doctor, Martin, had been wounded and was taking a brief rest upstairs where a roof beam had collapsed on a cupboard. The house was hit again now and more of the wounded were killed where they lay in the garden room. When the dust began to settle, others had disappeared. About this time another of the dressing stations, the Taffelberg Hotel, was hit again by shellfire and a nurse and two orderlies as well as wounded were killed. Warrack, going to see what he could do, found the place still under fire and rapidly becoming a shambles and thereupon did his best to get the wounded out. Orderlies began to take out the injured troops on wheelbarrow, trolleys, handcarts – anything with wheels. And the hospital buildings were hit again and again.

During the afternoon the Germans continued to infiltrate into the perimeter. One group took over a wood some two hundred yards away from the Hartenstein and it was noticed that they had a machine-gun at a point along one of the escape routes. They had to be shifted. Loder-Symonds therefore called up a shoot from the 64th Medium who bombarded this area, which was plumb in the middle of our perimeter, from a range of some 15,000 yards. He directed them from the roof of a high building on the far side of the target. I am sure there has never been such a fantastic shoot.

Meantime, Warrack was making efforts to clear yet another hospital building. On his rounds with a German doctor – the building was in German hands – he persuaded the German that one of the patients, my ADC, Graham Roberts, was unfit to be moved, having already seen to it that Roberts' leg was made to look a much bigger mess than it was by the attachment of long splints. Warrack had earlier come upon Roberts and another officer, Tony Murray, who had been lucky to survive a bullet through the neck, planning evasion. He had told them of the evacuation plan and now wanted them to deliver a signal requesting the gunners to take it easy while he completed the evacuation of his wounded from certain hospital buildings which were right in the target area.

As the two disabled officers set out, Roberts was slightly worried about the Pegasus pennant from my jeep which he carried in his pocket. It might be incriminating if he were taken prisoner. Nonetheless, he decided to keep it as a souvenir. My other pennant, a red Pegasus on a lance which it was my custom to place outside my tent or caravan on exercises in England, was outside the rear door of the Hartenstein. I had stuck it there when the battle became hot. From time to time during the battle it had been blasted into angles other than the perpendicular. And on this last afternoon of our battle I saw that it had been blown down. When I looked a short time later, someone had stood it up again.

As the fighting went on, so did the preparations for our getaway. Guides surreptitiously familiarized themselves with the selected routes. Tape was laid. Myers went to the waterside to supervise the ferrying. Loder-Symonds, in his compact garden tower behind the hotel, was tying up his arrangements for the artillery support while coping also with immediate demands for shoots. In the cellar of the Hartenstein, the sergeant clerk had started to type two copies of the division's war diary: he would carry one copy, an officer the other. To the east, our bombers were giving other Germans something else to think about. And from the Hartenstein Lieutenant Hardy, one of our signals officers, released the last of the carrier pigeons we had brought. One of these birds presently reached VIII Corps carrying Hardy's message:

Have to release birds owing to shortage of food and water. About eight tanks lying about in sub-unit areas, very untidy but not otherwise causing us any trouble. Now using as many German weapons as we have British. MGs most effective when aiming towards Germany. Dutch people grand but Dutch tobacco rather stringy. Great beard-growing competition on in our unit, but no time to check up on the winner.

During the day, Graeme Warrack had decided that one of

his doctors should be evacuated in order to pass on the specialist picture of the medical situation to the chief doctor at corps, Brigadier Eagger. His two former patients, Graham Roberts, and Tony Murray, in the meantime had walked out of the dressing station, collected two blankets and a medical pannier and gone out past the German guard. Beyond the outhouse where men who had died from their wounds had been placed, they knew there was a Red Cross jeep. They resisted a temptation to collect weapons from the pile taken from the wounded. Unchallenged, they reached the jeep and started it up.

They drove fast despite the treacherous obstacles on the road. It was getting dark now, and they didn't want to be late.

There was little time left. The Germans had made fresh inroads and in some places sections of the division were separated from the rest. We made our final preparations. The German prisoners had become an embarrassment. They would obviously take the first chance of breaking the news about our withdrawal, and as this was likely to be known to them long before daylight, at least a skeleton guard was needed. Military Police volunteers offered to stay and take their own chances of escape.

The night was made for clandestine exits. It was very dark with an inky sky and there was a strong wind and persistent heavy rain. In their muddy ditches and foxholes and slit trenches, saturated men found themselves glad of the rain which would deaden the noise and help our chances. They ticked off the minutes until it was their time to move.

From miles away across the river, the guns of XXX Corps opened up. Someone came into the Hartenstein cellar and said: 'It seems to be going all right.' We blackened our faces with ashes and mud and muffled our boots and any equipment, such as bayonets, which might rattle. Hancock produced some curtain material and helped me to wrap it round my boots.

In the Hartenstein, the padre entered the congested cellar from which we would soon depart. Like all the other padres and doctors, he was staying behind. We knelt in silent disarray where we had been standing, as he said a prayer.

At the river, Myers was marshalling the parties of fourteen into the boats. An anti-aircraft battery of the 43rd was firing red tracer shells over the two river routes as a further guide to the parties of men who were now making their hazardous and uncomfortable way down the escape lines. The immense artillery programme had started, and small-arms fire also covered the waters. Downstream beyond our perimeter the Dorsets who had crossed the night before to help us were still in action. In the fast-running river the storm boats were caught by the strong current and some were taken off course and drifted too far down. Others stalled, and the men used their rifles as oars. But already some boats had reached the far bank and were now returning for more men.

Some parties lost their way, and had difficulty in getting back on the routes. Others ran into Germans. Wilson's party was broken up by sudden Spandau fire, and there were casualties. Lieutenant-Colonel Gerald Mobbs, the divisional chief ordnance officer, was badly wounded during the withdrawal and eventually captured.

Along the two escape routes the groups of departing men held hands or each other's smocks to avoid losing touch. Silently, they passed the lengths of parachute tape tied to the trees. They passed the glider pilots, anonymous figures who put out guiding hands in the gloom to steer parties in the right direction. They passed close, many of them, to Mrs Ter Horst's house by the river, which was still full of wounded whose bandages now included table linen and silks, and their bedding civilian coats. Now and then a soldier broke his journey to call at the house and offer to take a wounded comrade. Out of the night came a soldier bent on collecting his wounded captain whom he had delivered at the house some days before. The captain, thinking he would be too great a burden, refused to go; a glider pilot, less badly injured, took up the offer.

The time for our going from the Hartenstein was close. The padre bade us Godspeed. We burned all our papers. In my pack I found a forgotten bottle of whisky. I handed it round; everyone in the party, I think had a nip. The sergeant-major, still careful about equal shares, distributed benzedrine pills.

I put mine in a pocket intending to take them, but forgot. Finally, I went among the wounded lying in the cellars in their bloody bandages and crude splints and said goodbye to those who were aware of what was happening. Others, morphia-injected, were mercifully out of it. I wished them well, and one worn-out soldier, propping himself against the cellar wall, murmured, 'I hope you make it, sir.'

Then we left in single file with Mackenzie leading followed by Gordon Grieve. Graham Roberts was with us and so was Hancock who had disappeared for a few moments. Unknown to me, he had gone outside to untie my Pegasus pennant which was now inside his battledress blouse. Fortified spiritually by the padre, and physically by the whisky, we made our way through the rain and the mud under the dripping trees. Although the distance was short, it seemed much greater and to take a long time. Once we heard voices coming from a German post and there was a whispered conference about the advisability of throwing a grenade. Mortar bursts and small-arms fire made us stop from time to time. Presently we reached the marshland and followed the guide line of parachute tape along a ditch to the waterside. On the river bank lay parties of troops who had arrived before us: patiently they lay in the ooze waiting for their turn. They were quiet and orderly and in good heart despite their exhaustion.

As we pressed ourselves into the mud I watched more parties waiting and arriving and as my eyes became accustomed to the dark, this and the light from the steady tracer showed figures making their way towards the river. In spite of the decision that men who could not walk had to be left, I saw wounded men who couldn't be described as walking cases being assisted by their comrades to the bank. Badly injured men, some of whom had come by their wounds only in the last few minutes on the way down the routes, were being lifted into the boats.

Eddie Myers moved about the bank embarking parties as rapidly as he could and Mackenzie, who had slipped off to see what was happening at the other crossing point, returned to tell me that the delay we were now experiencing was due to the sinking of something like half of the boats within the first hour. As these losses were understandably not distributed equally between the two crossings, some reorganization had been necessary. And as Myers now did his best to compensate for the lost craft by swift turn rounds and efficient loading, soldiers lay in the churned ground whispering witticisms. A mortar bomb landed some twenty yards away. Another followed. The chugging of the storm boats' engines sounded alarmingly loud and now and then we could near splashing as men scrambled aboard, or started to swim from sinking craft.

It seemed we lay there for hours.

Then, from out of the night came a subdued voice: 'Right – this party.' I looked at my watch. It was a few minutes past midnight. We collected ourselves and slid down the banking. By the light of the tracer I could see other boats dimly through the rain. I climbed aboard from the sodden, slippery groyne. It was a tight squeeze and the boat was low in the water. There was an exclamation from the Canadian sapper who was running this ferry, and from the disgusted tone it was plain that all was not well. We had, in fact, stuck in the mud. Someone slipped over the side to push us off. It was my diminutive batman, Hancock. He got us clear and as the boat moved slowly out and into the deeper water Hancock was still holding on. He struggled to get aboard again and some other occupant shouted down to him: 'Let go! It's overcrowded already.' Irked by such ingratitude, Hancock ignored the remark and summoning his last reserves pulled himself into the boat.

Spandaus covered the river and metal splashed into the water as we seemed to go all too slowly across the two hundred yards towards the south bank. We were about half way over when the engine gave out. There was an urgent exchange between the ferryman and one of our party and there were confused efforts to restart the engine. The boat drifted in the strong current. It was only for a few minutes, but it seemed an absolute age before we were on our way again. From the din and the great flashes of light it was obvious that the XXX Corps gunners were doing a powerful job and that they were probably making all the difference between a catastrophic evacuation and a successful one. High up on Westerbouwing there were flashes from where the Germans were firing indiscriminately on the expanse of water below.

Suddenly the boat bumped alongside a groyne, veered round and a voice croaked, 'All right. Let's be having you.' We climbed out, sinking in the ooze. I could make out dim silhouettes on the rising ground in front. I followed them over the banking and across a hundred yards of muddy marsh to the foot of the dyke wall. All around men were scrambling over. I took a grip, dug my right boot into the scarred concrete and heaved. As I rose there was an ominous snap. 'Blast!' I murmured and the voice of Graham Roberts came out of the gloom nearby solemnly inquiring whether I was intact.

'It's all right,' I said. 'It's only my braces.'

Even in these circumstances, when my chief reaction was one of heartfelt relief, it was an annoying indignity.

When we set out down the road beyond the dyke, I was holding my trousers up.

The ferrying went on through the rainstorm.

As more parties arrived at the north bank, they took their turn for the boats. Everyone was remarkably calm. The long odds brought out the best in men. There were cases of soldiers giving up their places in the boats to others in worse shape. Wounded men were appearing in the boats and on the south bank. And in the perimeter other wounded, with not a hope of escaping, kept up with the rearguard parties the pretence that the area was still occupied. They fired everything they could lay hands on, and the wireless sets were worked.

More boats were lost. One capsized after running into a mudbank and its occupants, including Boy Wilson, struck out and swam for it. On the north bank, officers and men voluntarily and spontaneously took it upon themselves to speed the evacuation by organizing and dispatching stragglers separated from their parties by the darkness or German intervention. At 1.30 am the skeleton guard quietly withdrew from the POW cage once they knew that no other members of the division remained north of the Hartenstein. The little ammunition that was left was blown up. After one such act of destruction which rocked the house next to Oosterbeek

Church, a soldier found the time to call in order to reassure the wounded housed there that the bang was nothing to worry about. Close by, the Light Regiment's remaining guns fired their last shells. Methodically, the gunners removed the breech blocks and sights and took them to the river for dumping. The gunners were among the last to leave and as the first grey light of dawn revealed to the Germans the loophole through which their prey had escaped a boat was hit and sunk.

There were still hundreds of men left on the north bank. The last ferry had gone.

Now came the awful choice. Many officers and men plunged into the swift waters and were swept away; some were dragged down by the weight of their clothes and equipment. Others now stripped naked and dived, and many of them got over. Among them was Major Linton. They found clothing in the houses on the south side. One officer was wrapped in yards of flannel held by a Sam Browne and another swimmer, RSM Seely, appeared in a woman's coat.

As the last swimmers took to the water, German tanks were rolling into the perimeter. In Mrs Ter Horst's house by the river, the wounded who had heard all the comings and goings now lay and listened to the clanking tracks of the Tigers and the weird sighs that were like a last gasp. Then they heard the crash of the tank guns. Taking no chances, the tank commander was putting shots into the houses along the southern road. Accompanied by the padre, the medical orderly, Bombardier Bolden, now went out and asked the German tank officer to respect the house.

As we strode out along the road beyond the dyke, Roberts and I were challenged in the dark by a familiar voice. It was that of Colonel Henniker, the 43rd Division's chief engineer who had previously been with the 1st Airborne Division. He was wearing a ground sheet, and a tin hat to keep off the rain. He appeared to be optimistic about the progress of the evacuation. We kept going down the road until we reached the HQ of the leading brigade of the 43rd Division. I went in with Roberts and asked them to pass on news of our arrival.

When we came outside the blacked-out cottage HQ again,

I could see the fireworks display over the perimeter area and I wondered how many of my troops would emerge safely through this night. I had lost touch even with those in my boat, except for Roberts. Hancock had vanished. He was, in fact, having quite a night. After climbing the dyke wall, he had been directed across the fields when he saw in the pale glare from the tracers and shell-bursts what he took to be a tarmacadam road. He thought it would not be so far on his feet. He discovered, too late, that it was a ditch and the glint he had seen had come off the water. Hancock had to swim for it and presently he got out on the other side and headed towards Nijmegen where he hoped to find my caravan, which had arrived with the seaborne tail of the division, consisting of some thousand vehicles.

Down the road towards Driel, Roberts and I came upon General Thomas's tactical HQ. I sent Roberts inside to fix up some transport to our own Corps HQ, for I was keen to get back as soon as possible to report to General Browning. I chose to stay outside. When Roberts appeared in the basement room they occupied, the staff officers displayed some surprise. He had several days' growth of beard, his battledress was torn and stained with blood and he was, of course, as unwashed and just as smelly as the rest of us. He was not received with any warmth.

We had not been there long when Browning's ADC, Harry Cator, turned up in a jeep and drove us back himself through the pouring rain. When we reached Browning's HQ I felt extremely tired and was very wet. I was too tired even to sit down as Cator showed us into a tidy room with a framed photograph of a German general on one wall. It hung slightly askew and the glass was broken. Castor explained that Browning had self-expressively thrown an inkpot at it.

Browning was a little time coming, but when he did appear he was as usual immaculately turned out. He looked as if he had just come off parade instead of from his bed in the middle of a battle. I tried to display some briskness as I reported: 'The division is nearly out now. I'm sorry we haven't been able to do what we set out to do.'

Browning offered me a drink and assured me that

everything was being done for the division. 'You did all you could,' he said. 'Now you had better get some rest.'

It was a totally inadequate meeting, but my mind had already seized up and every thought required an effort of willpower. I was still soaked and Cator sent round some spare suits of battledress to the room I was allocated in the house next door to that occupied by Browning. An orderly brought me a cup of tea. I took off my equipment and lay down on a bed that was too comfortable. Sleep did not come easily. Through my head images tumbled over each other in a confusion of memories and ideas and plans. Behind them all the big questions looked like some bewildering backcloth. Could we have been quicker off the mark at the beginning? What had become of Frost? What had happened to our fighter support? What had kept XXX Corps? How many officers and men of the division had got out? The questions were logical enough, yet oddly they seemed to belong to another life. They hung there in space.

When I got up I found that someone had pinched my razor from the small kit which I had left in the bathroom. This seemed the last straw! I drove to the rendezvous near Driel where the 43rd Division had collected the survivors and given them tea, a hot meal, blankets and cigarettes. Many of them were still outside the reception building and Charles Mackenzie, aware that they were exposed to the Germans occupying the high ground north of the river, realized that they would have to be moved rapidly. Accordingly, he got them on the road towards Nijmegen. There was transport for most of them, but some walked wearily on.

There was no last-minute tragedy.

Across the river, in what had been the perimeter, Graeme Warrack and his medical staff searched for the wounded. As he went to the Hartenstein Hotel, Warrack was saddened by the desolation and it seemed that there were only dead airborne soldiers and swarms of live Germans. Silence had settled over the area, broken only by the intermittent bursts of small-arms fire as unwilling stragglers refused to surrender when cornered. Near one house Warrack found a group of soldiers who had been killed by a shellburst; among them one man still lived, both his legs broken. In other houses he found more wounded. He gave them morphia and applied splints. Already, however, the Germans had found and were collecting most of the wounded, but Warrack commandeered a jeep from a German private and scoured the two escape routes. The Germans were using thirty-six ambulances painted white and bearing large Red Crosses.

Outside the house next door to Oosterbeek Church, Mrs Ter Horst loaded a handcart which had somehow remained intact. Escorted to the German command post across the road, she had been ordered by the senior officer present to get out of the area. Her efforts on our behalf had not gone unremarked by the Germans. She put her children and three bags on the cart and, with a friend, set out for a destination that she had not clearly decided. There were friends on a farm in the north and she might try to reach them. The journey would last for days. As she started now, pushing the frail cart, the British walking wounded were being assembled near the village concert hall.

She hardly dared look in their direction as she passed.

On both sides of the Neder Rhine on this morning of September 26th, 1944, officers were working out the reckoning. In addition to the very large numbers of men in the dressing stations, some 300 wounded were picked up inside the perimeter along with 200 Dorsets. The Germans, it was being freely said, had lost 7000 men in the fight for Arnhem. In houses and cottages, ditches and woodland, and in the crowded wards of hospitals, men of the 1st Airborne Division were planning to escape. About 200 evaders were at large, hiding themselves or being hidden by brave civilians who knew only too well the cost of discovery.

South of the river, the heads were counted. They gave an accurate picture of the ultimate reckoning. Out of 8905 officers and men who had landed, plus 1100 glider pilots, 2163 of us had come back – with 160 Poles and seventy-five Dorsets. From Arnhem and Oosterbeek more than 1200 officers and men of the 1st Airborne Division and the Glider Pilot Regiment would never return.

It was not quite all over yet.

# CHAPTER EIGHT

I was not yet ready to analyse the battle, nor even inclined to look back in anger or regret at the causes of this tragic yet inspiring operation of war through which we had just lived. Apart from the fact that most of the vital witnesses were either dead or wounded in German hands, I shared with other survivors of the division an incredible lassitude that was to persist for weeks so that it required a conscious effort to attend to routine matters which normally I would have taken in my stride. Certainly on that first day south of the river nothing could have been further from my mind than the thought that the 2nd Army's failure to establish a bridgehead north of the Neder Rhine at this stage of the war, would have tremendous significance in terms of the duration of the war in Europe. Monty, Eisenhower and the Allies were now committed to a winter on the doorstep of Germany; gone was the opportunity to race across the north German plain!

I paid the usual courtesy calls on those who had been closest to us in the battle – General Horrocks at XXX Corps; General Thomas of the 43rd Division, and the 64th Medium Regiment, whose gunners had sustained such brilliantly accurate long-distance shooting in our interests, and but for whom we would almost surely have been wiped out. The commander of the 64th, Lieutenant-Colonel Hunt, was away when I called and I mentioned to his second-in-command that I considered that their shooting had earned them the right to wear the Pegasus arm badge of Airborne Forces. Presently I was to make strong representations in this direction but the War Office remained adamant in refusing to allow any such gesture to be made.

With my troops now comfortably housed in three school buildings at Nijmegen I returned to Browning's HQ and started to dictate letters of thanks to those who had given us support and co-operation, including the RAF and the Americans. Usually, I can dictate fairly freely, but my brain had seized up so that I was incapable of framing even the most simple observations. Finally, Browning's secretary considerately suggested that he might write the letters. They were rather formal and certainly did not express the deeply-felt gratitude I would have liked to convey.

On this first evening since the evacuation, Browning's staff laid on a party to celebrate our return. They invited Horrocks. When I went up to my room to rest before getting ready for it, I was surprised to find Hancock back. He was grinning hugely as he told me of his adventures. He had brought my spare battledress from my caravan which he had found in the Nijmegen area, and where he had stolen a few hours' sleep on my bed.

'I hope you found it very comfortable,' I told him.

'Oh, I did, sir.' Then: 'I thought you'd like this,' and with the air of an actor throwing away his best line he produced from his battledress blouse my Pegasus pennant.

The dinner party was an extravagant affair for those days, with chicken and plenty of wine. It was an ordeal even to have to face such food, let alone consume it. My system had got out of the way of eating and I remember glancing at Graham Roberts and Robert Loder-Symonds and wondering if they felt as queasy as I felt. I also found it hard to take in what was being said about the battle, much as I wanted to find out from Horrocks especially what had kept XXX Corps so long. From time to time during the evening I was aware that he was doing his stuff in the way I had come to know on an earlier visit to his HQ. It was his habit to work on anyone with his hands, his eyes and his voice, and in the process he tended to get closer and closer to his victim. I remembered this hypnotic technique on one of the occasions when I flew to his HQ on the Continent to discuss a previous airborne operation in conjunction with his corps, which never materialized. As he was talking to me, his hands were waving up and down in a vertical plane in front of my face and I was fixed with his stare and a rapid exposition of what he wished to put across. He always tended towards the theatrical and perhaps it was a useful asset for a commander of his kind for there was no doubt that he was able to put himself over in an excellent way, and he was particularly good talking to troops. On this night, however, I found his hypnosis far from soothing and I could not help wondering why XXX Corps had been so slow and unaware of the urgency when they had a commander with such a capacity for dynamic human relations.

I noticed, too, that Horrocks, Browning and Harry Cator all were apparently enjoying healthy appetites. The food nauseated me. The battle still raged in my head.

It was a relief when the party ended.

By now, the battlefield north of the river had been cleared. Earlier in the day, there was an uplifting moment for the British wounded in the St Elizabeth Hospital when they heard troops singing on the march and discovered, as the singing grew louder and the words distinguishable, that those singing were their wounded comrades from the perimeter. There were some 500 exhausted men, some limping and on sticks, some swathed in bandages which were now a filthy brown colour and caked in the dirt in which they had fought. Their faces were bearded and sunken and their eyes red raw from sleeplessness. Yet they sang on the march, and the Dutch civilians who were now being forced out of their homes looked on and marvelled, and the Germans were awed. There were many who witnessed this strange sight who say that the men looked unbeatable and that it was more like a victory march.

Reporting on the battle, Sturmbannführer Sepp Krafft, commander of the reserve battalion which had done so much to delay us on the first day, described the troops of the 1st Airborne Division as 'about twenty-five years of age on the average, and the best type, mentally and physically. They all had some five or six years' service and most of them were veterans of North Africa, Sicily, Italy and Normandy. They were well trained, particularly for independent fighting and of good combat value. The officers, graded up in rank according to age, were the finest in the whole British Army. Very well schooled, personally hard, persevering and brave, they made an outstanding impression.'

Under the heading of 'Political Convictions', Krafft wrote:

Not much information has been gleaned, but it is known that, in England, when the truth conflicts with the military powers, the truth is withheld. In this respect, chalked inscriptions on the gliders are interesting:

> We are the Al Capone Gang
> Up with the Reds
> Up with the frauleins skirts

How far this is connected with the political convictions of the troops themselves or whether it is due to Bolshevist or American influence, is not known.

The Germans were behaving with correctness and in some instances with extreme helpfulness. Warrack and his medical officers wondered how much of this was due to the imminence of Allied victory and the inevitable reckoning, and how much to their respect for the tremendous fight put up by the division. By early evening, some 900 wounded British troops were being settled into a barracks at Apeldoorn which was to be their hospital. Already about 500 lightly wounded men had passed through on their way into Germany as prisoners-of-war. With Warrack and his twenty-four medical officers at the hospital were 180 RAMC medical orderlies and stretcher-bearers as well as a number of Dutch nurses who had been working in the dressing stations. It was a cold and unfriendly place and the conditions were primitive: the wounded lay on the floors, some of them on straw, and there were not enough blankets to go round. The 'meal' consisted of brown bread and a watery stew.

In Arnhem and Oosterbeek more than two hundred officers and men were making their escape plans. Some were in St Elizabeth Hospital, including Hackett whose condition was too serious to allow him to be removed; others had escaped from the hospital, including Lathbury who had walked out on the night of September 25th and had gone into hiding in the woods. There were still more evaders in the woods around Arnhem and Oosterbeek and even farther afield in country houses and huts and outhouses and attics. Altogether, there were more than 250 officers and men of the division on the run. And they were being watched over by the men and women of the Dutch Resistance, of which unfortunately we did not make enough use while the battle was on. Among the escapers were Digby Tatham-Warter, who had set such an example during the fighting at the Bridge and who had also got away from hospital, and David Dobie, the young commander of the 1st Parachute Battalion who had been wounded in the eye and arm and had been captured on the third day.

In the red-brick school back at Nijmegen, the survivors of the Division were paraded and Boy Browning spoke successively in each of the three buildings. He congratulated them on the show they had put up, and gave them the big picture of the entire operation. On the Thursday I lunched with General Dempsey at 2nd Army HQ and then went on to stay with Monty at his tactical HQ near Eindhoven. It was around teatime when we arrived, and one of Monty's aides, Johnny Henderson, was worried because two of the Field-Marshal's pet rabbits had escaped.

Monty greeted me with that brisk radiance which so characterized him. If the result of the operation was not to his liking – and it could not have been – he did not show any disappointment. 'Good to see you got back all right,' he said, extending his hand. 'Come and sit down and let's talk it over.' He indicated two canvas chairs outside his caravan. It was one of those warm, clear afternoons when the drone of distant aircraft may be heard. His ADC handed him a marked map, which he placed across our knees and I described our battle north of the Neder Rhine. I pointed out the places where we had run into trouble on the western edge of Arnhem, and the area round Wolfhezen where Hackett had met such opposition in trying to come down to us from the north.

Monty asked me a lot of questions, but he had few observations to make, and certainly appeared to think that we had done all we could. We had dinner in his mess tent and, before going off to bed, at his usual early hour, Monty said: 'By the way, you'd better go home in my personal aircraft.' During the day I had received a signal from Paul Williams, the American general commanding the 9th US Troop Carrier Command, offering to send his aircraft to Brussels to pick me up and fly me back to England. I suggested to Monty

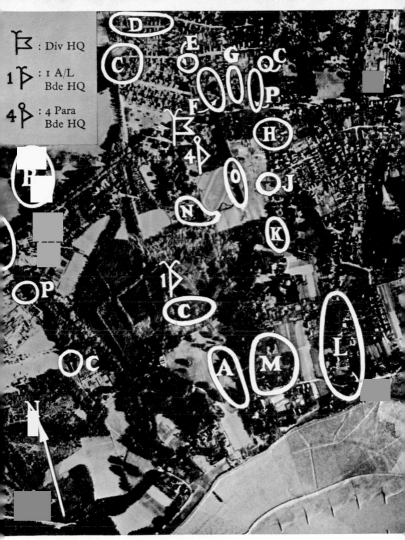

## THE PERIMETER JUST BEFORE WE WITHDREW

A  Companies of 1st Border Regt
B  9th Field Coy, RE
C  Glider Pilot Regt detachments
D  7th KOSB
E  1st A/L Recce Sqdn
F  156th Para Bn
G  10th Para Bn

H  21st Ind Para Coy
J  4th Para Bde HQ Composite Platoon
K  RASC
L  Lonsdale Force (Elements 1st, 3rd
   and 11th Para Bns and South Staffs)
M  Div Arty
N  Div HQ troops
P  Dets of 1st Polish Para Bde

HOUSE CLEARING IN OOSTERBEEK

GERMAN TROOPS FERRETED OUT BY PARATROOPERS

MAJOR ROBERT CAIN, VC

CAPTAIN L.E. QUERIPEL, VC

LIEUTENANT J.H. GRAYBURN, VC

SERGEANT J.D. BASKERFIELD, VC

FLIGHT LIEUTENANT D.S.A. LORD, VC

MUCH OF THE RE-SUPPLY WENT TO THE GERMANS

FIELD-MARSHAL MODEL                    THE AUTHOR

that it might be more tactful if I were to accept Williams's offer. 'By all means I think you should,' Monty replied.

Next morning I was taking an early breather before leaving when Monty came out of his caravan flourishing a piece of paper. 'This I would like to give you,' he said. 'I shall issue a copy to my public relations officer as well.' The letter was typewritten but Monty said he had written it that morning in his own hand.

It was not until some time later when we were aboard the aircraft taking us to Brussels that I had an opportunity to read it:

Major-Gen R. E. Urquhart,
Comd, 1 Airborne Division.

I want to express to you personally, and to every officer and man in your Division, my appreciation of what you all did at Arnhem for the Allied cause.

I also want to express to you my own admiration, and the admiration of us all in 21 Army Group, for the magnificent fighting spirit that your Division displayed in battle against great odds on the north bank of the Lower Rhine in Holland.

There is no shadow of doubt that, had you failed, operations elsewhere would have been gravely compromised. You did not fail and all is well elsewhere.

I would like all Britain to know that in your final message from the Arnhem area you said:

'All will be ordered to break out rather than surrender. We have attempted our best, and we will continue to do our best as long as possible.'

And all Britain will say to you:

'You did your best; you all did your duty; and we are proud of you.'

In the annals of the British Army there are many glorious deeds. In our Army we have always drawn great strength and inspiration from past traditions, and endeavoured to live up to the high standards of those who have gone before.

But there can be few episodes more glorious than the epic of Arnhem, and those that follow after will find it hard to live up to the standards that you have set.

So long as we have in the armies of the British Empire officers and men who will do as you have done, then we can indeed look forward with complete confidence to the future.

In years to come it will be a great thing for a man to be able to say:

'I fought at Arnhem.'

Please give my best wishes and my grateful thanks to every officer and man in your Division.

In the Field.                                                B. L. Montgomery

When we reached Brussels, the remnants of the Division had already arrived at Louvain preparatory to their return to England, and as there was room for more in Williams's aircraft we took aboard a number of glider pilots. From the moment when we were welcomed at Cranwell by General Brereton, the Allied Airborne Army commander, and Major-General Crawford, the Director of Land-Air Warfare in the War Office, life became a whirl of interviews and appointments. I reported to the War Office and saw the CIGS, Sir Alan Brooke. Then I was summoned to Buckingham Palace where King George VI gave me a CB and asked me for a brief account of the battle. There was a frighteningly large press conference, with reporters from all over the world. I was also bidden to visit Queen Wilhelmina of the Netherlands.

With Roberts, I went to the country house near Slough to which she had been temporarily exiled by the war. We were shown into a large and sunny room containing many photographs and when the Queen entered with a lady-in-waiting I was impressed by her. 'We are all most grateful for what you have done for our country,' she said. 'Your men have been very courageous.' She was unwilling to hear anything less than the truth: she made no effort to conceal her anxiety for her people and for the men we had left behind. Roberts mentioned the dressing stations and the excellent work done there by the Dutch nurses.

'What do you think has become of them?' the Queen asked.

'Well, ma'am, they were wearing Red Cross uniforms, so no doubt they will be all right,' Roberts replied comfortingly.

The Queen turned sharply and her voice was full of innuendo. 'And do you really think the Germans respect the Red Cross?'

I told her of the wonderful support we had been given by the Resistance men and women, and of the destruction in Arnhem and Oosterbeek and of the regrettable civilian casualties.

'I should like to express my country's gratitude with some decorations,' she said. 'I think they ought to be made right away.'

There were difficulties in the way of accepting foreign decorations. According to War Office policy, every Dutch decoration given a British soldier had to be matched by a British award to someone in the Dutch Army. The same problem arose over the question of decorations from the United States and Poland, who also wished to honour members of the division. I was also hampered by the fact that so few commanders had returned. The two parachute brigadiers – Lathbury and Hackett – had both been left wounded; Hicks had returned with me. Of the nine battalion commanders, Fitch, des Voeux and Smyth were dead; Frost, Lea, McCardie and Hadden were prisoners, and Dobie had yet to escape. Only Payton-Reid came out. Sheriff Thompson, who knew all about the performance of the Light Regiment on that fated rising ground in Oosterbeek, was wounded – and the doctors had stayed to a man.

I wanted to be sure that officers and men unrepresented by any of those who survived should be given proper consideration. Not surprisingly, for he looked after his men, Hackett had begun to prepare a list of officers and men who had earned awards even as he lay in a serious condition after the operation on his stomach. And presently I received via the Dutch Underground several laboriously pencilled pages dated October 9th, 1944, and headed 'Recommendation for Awards'. There followed notes on a number of officers and men and the things they had done at Arnhem, as well as a general account of what had happened to our wounded. 'I hope these things get through and that I follow them shortly myself. Thank you for the party. It didn't go quite as we hoped and got a bit rougher than we expected, but speaking for myself I'd take it on again any time and so I'm sure would everyone else.'

There was a postscript in which Hackett related how he had been 'making up some kit against the future' with the Padre's help and wanted a stick. 'I suddenly saw one abandoned in a corner. I bagged it and then saw it was none other than that one with a U carved on it about which we had such an ugly scene, when I made probably quite unfounded accusations that you had pinched it! I brought it out with me and shall probably be in a position to give it back to you before long.' He kept his word!

Hackett left the hospital with help from the Dutch patriots. A number of these Resistance groups were now at work helping the evaders, and many of their members were incredibly young – teenagers of both sexes. David Dobie, walking along the Ede road after narrowly escaping recapture near the river, was led by a young blonde girl into hiding in her father's house. Sergeant-Major Grainger, who with two other soldiers had masqueraded as mental patients and had even danced and grimaced for the benefit of German troops past whom they were led, had presently been given refuge in a house at Ede and was to be seen around the town with a Dutch girl. Lathbury, after wandering around the woods for ten days, was taken under cover by a Resistance leader named Bill. Graeme Warrack, when he had decided that he could do no more for the wounded, walled himself up in his office to avoid being taken back into Germany and then escaped from the Apeldoorn hospital in his own time. He was hidden in a cottage after being welcomed inside by two good-looking young girls.

And even after the Germans had evacuated the entire civilian population of Arnhem, young Resistance men were still visiting the St Elizabeth Hospital. One of them was called Blue Johnny, a boy of about seventeen with a crew-cut and wearing blue jeans who produced comforts such as a chess set and a tiny bottle of brandy; his real name was Zwerus de Noofj and he was a nephew of three old ladies under whose roof Hackett was soon to be sheltered. Another visitor to the hospital was known as Piet and he told Hackett: 'I know who you are and I can help you get out of here.' Hackett, on his guard, replied that he didn't know what Piet was talking about. The Dutchman, who was slim, with bright eyes and a turned-up nose, later brought a note in Lathbury's hand: 'You can trust Piet. He helped me out of the hospital. Put yourself in his hands, and I reckon he can help you.'

Meanwhile, a padre of the 4th Parachute Brigade, Danny McGowan, was taking shopping lists and visiting the glider landing zones to pick up such necessities of life as malted milk tablets and escape outfits. The sight of his red beret was said to be enough to give the Germans fits. When he tried to make his own escape and was caught on the bank of the Rhine the Germans beat him up mainly out of their fear of the red beret. His protests that he was a priest only angered them more. It was bad enough that he should be a Red Devil, let alone that he should claim priestly status. McGowan's shopping trips finally produced all Hackett needed for his break-out and one day Blue Johnny brought a suit of civilian clothes.

He had come upon a group of Germans looting a house.

'What are you doing here?' he demanded imperiously.

'Helping ourselves,' they retorted.

He pretended that it was his own home and said mock-submissively: 'I can't do anything about it, I suppose. Perhaps you will let me take a suitcase and some clothes.'

'Help yourself.'

Shortly afterwards, at the height of a raid by the RAF, Piet appeared and told Hackett to follow. On the way they called at the mortuary where the Resistance kept its arms, removed a blood-caked bandage from a corpse, and Piet fitted it round Hackett's head. A car waited outside. Piet shouted at the German sentry: 'Casualty! Badly wounded! Taking him to hospital!'

Apparently it did not occur to the sentry that the 'casualty' was being taken away from the hospital.

Hackett was delivered into the care of four old ladies who nursed him through the months that followed in their house at Ede.

By this time, the village of Ede was a veritable honeycomb

of British hideouts. It was estimated that about 100 members of the division were in the place, another fifty on the outskirts, with a hundred or so more around Arnhem.

Lathbury was at Ede, and so were Dobie, Tatham-Warter and an officer named Franks. It seemed at times that the division was re-forming there. And in the hope that the 2nd Army would still cross the river, this group of survivors thought out a scheme whereby they might ambush roads leading to any bridgehead Dempsey might create. They had their own operations room in a cellar, and there they planned to equip the little force with Brens, Piats and anti-tank mines which would be dropped to them by night. Soon, they were active in passing information to the 2nd Army gunners whose subsequent shoots caused the Germans no little consternation, and to the 2nd Tactical Air Force whose Typhoon pilots were given specific targets including a military train.

All this time, the clandestine group was using the Dutch telephone service.

When it became obvious that the 2nd Army were not likely to cross the river for some time, a mass escape was planned. For this, the 2nd Army's help was required and Lathbury sent Dobie over the river to Dempsey's HQ. The Germans were becoming increasingly suspicious of the happenings in Ede and a contingent of SS presently arrived in the village. Dobie was passed from one house to another in the Underground chain: he was rowed across the Rhine and on the following night shared a boat with another Resistance man across the Waal. He reached Dempsey's HQ on October 19th, carrying plans, photographs and other information of use to the 2nd Army and Dempsey agreed that the Airborne troops around Ede should be brought back. Dobie worked out an idea to accomplish this with General Horrocks. They had two crossings in mind, but had to be satisfied with one after hearing on the telephone from Ede that the Germans were now much more busy and that any further delay would be risky. The escape was fixed for the night of October 22nd.

Everyone reached the rendezvous. Major Tony Hibbert and some twenty others, arriving by lorry, were urged out of the way as they climbed down by a party of German cyclists which was passing at the time. Other airborne troops turned up from houses in the neighbourhood and thirty parachutists, in full uniform and armed, reached the bank of the river from Velp, another airborne harbour. Lathbury was among the party. Presently, after an eternity of waiting, they were hailed by an American voice. Half an hour later, all were safe on the south bank. It was a triumph for the Dutch Resistance workers, whose guides and couriers had made the operation possible.

A further 120 of my officers and men were out.

With many others still in hiding north of the river, Major Hugh Maguire led a second attempt some time afterwards. This time there were about a hundred people in the party including British and American airmen and Dutch doctors and nurses, John Coke, who was killed in the attempt, and Graeme Warrack. Most of them assembled in a barn and they had a long way to go. There were four main obstacles: two major roads, a side road and a railway line. As they moved stealthily towards the river, where red tracer was being fired over the crossing point, they were intercepted by German patrols. In the fighting that followed several of the party were killed and others were recaptured. Only seven got clear. Warrack survived to try again. Afterwards, it was obvious that the Germans had been prepared for the break, despite the most discreet operations of the Resistance, because of the earlier breakout and the extraordinary amount of publicity which it had been given.

There was the further handicap that many of the escapers were in no physical condition after so much hardship to face the rigours of a forced night march. From time to time liaison officers were passing down the line in order to round up stragglers and the column was delayed when some groups began to lose ground. Some of the troops, before being taken into the care of the Resistance, had walked for miles in their stockinged feet after their boots had been taken away by their captors as a deterrent to any escape ideas which they harboured.

And still there remained many who prepared for a further attempt. In the weeks and months that followed this ill-fated escape bid, officers and men were still finding their way back into the 2nd Army lines. There was the case of Major Tony

Deane-Drummond who was recaptured even after swimming the Neder Rhine, but then hid from the Germans by having himself shut up in a cupboard and remaining there for twelve days with a piece of bread and the contents of his water bottle. He made good his escape some weeks later. Others got out by canoe, being guided along the fast-flowing Waal by skilled Dutch guides. Warrack escaped this way. So did Hackett who in the interim had occupied his plentiful time by becoming 'Military Correspondent' to a clandestine newspaper. The technique was to embark in the canoes on the lower reaches of the Waal, along the northern shore close enough not to attract enemy fire from the southern side and out of sight of any German posts on the near bank above. When that part of the southern bank was reached which was in British hands, the canoes swung across the river. Some were wrecked in the fast waters during squalls, but many got away.

The British were warned by the Dutch Resistance to keep an eye open for canoeists at certain times. Hackett was received by an officer of the 11th Hussars carrying a bottle of brandy. He had arranged that once he had arrived safely he would have a message sent over Radio Orange: 'The grey goose is gone.' The old ladies who had cared for him so long switched on the set they kept under the floor and when they heard these words they danced round the table for joy.

As soon as Ede was liberated, Hackett flew over from Britain in an Oxford loaded with good things for those who at such risk had befriended the escaping airborne men. Even as the German rearguards were fighting at one side of the town, Hackett was renewing acquaintances at the other. He has kept up his friendships of those days steadily ever since – and so have hundreds of others in the division. The Cauldron forged lasting relationships between the soldiers and the civilian populations of Arnhem and Oosterbeek. Years after the events that caused them, they are as fresh and meaningful as ever. Men still call at the houses and shops where they fought so valiantly, and men and women of Arnhem and Oosterbeek visiting Britain look up the soldiers they met in those September days. The Arnhem Pilgrimage each year revives memories, and produces extraordinary encounters. In September 1957 a tall Dutch youth of nearly twenty recognized a glider pilot as the soldier who had given him sweets one morning as the 1st Airborne Division was marching into Arnhem in 1944.

As more and more officers and men rejoined the division, I was better able to reconstruct the battle in my own mind. The picture was becoming clear when I received a letter from SHAEF dated October 8th, 1944:

Dear General Urquhart:

The Chief of the Imperial General Staff has just informed me that, due to the great losses the First British Airborne Division suffered at Arnhem, it will probably not be possible to reconstitute it. This occasions me the same deep regret that I know you must feel, because in this war there has been no single performance by any unit that has more greatly inspired me or more highly excited my admiration, than the nine day action of your Division between September 17 and 26.

There is no question that these sentiments are shared by every soldier, sailor and airman of the entire Allied Expeditionary Force now battling toward the Rhine River.

Before the world the proud record that your Division has established needs no embellishment from me, but I should like every survivor of that gallant band to realize, not only how deeply this whole Command appreciates his example of courage, fortitude, and skill, but that the Division's great battle contributed effectively to the success of operations to the southward of its own battle-ground.

Your officers and men were magnificent. Pressed from every side, without relief, reinforcement or respite, they inflicted such losses on the Nazi that his infantry dared not close with them. In an unremitting hail of steel from German snipers, machine-guns, mortars, rockets, cannon of all calibers and self-propelled and tank artillery, they never flinched, never wavered. They held steadfastly.

For nine days they checked the furious assault of the Nazis and when, on 26th September, they were ordered to withdraw across the river, they came out a proud and haughty band – paratroopers, air-landing men, glider pilots, clerks, cooks and batmen, soldiers all – two thousand strong out of seven thousand five hundred that entered the battle.

The Allied Expeditionary Forces salute them.

My profound admiration and warm regards to you, personally,

Sincerely,

Dwight D. Eisenhower.

In January 1945 I made my official report and summed up the lessons of the operation. Nothing I have learned since has fundamentally altered my conclusions. In the first place, our distance from the objective when we landed was much too great. The DZs and LZs were too far away for anyone's liking. There were smaller areas nearer the town on which we could have landed a company or so, though the use of these would have involved the routing and diversion of aircraft from the main stream and the difficulty of persuading the airmen to fly into a flak-protected zone was always with us. Deelen airfield, a natural landing zone, came into this category, though it also was too far away. Doubtless, minor diversions could have been made but the flak area was reported to extend over a large area beyond the town. I think that not more than a few companies could have been landed very much nearer unless we had accepted a flight into the flak and the dropping of men in the polder country south of the bridge which was reported as unsuitable. Intelligence reports over the weeks before the drop had built up an extensive flak picture which tended to increase. This flak was taken on by fighters before the fly-in began, and on the day before, pilots on their way back from targets in Germany and other parts of Holland were told to strafe these areas.

In addition, the polder country was described as being unsuitable for the landing of gliders and also for their unloading, and the movement of jeeps and heavy equipment. This was a mistaken assessment. In fact, it would have been perfectly feasible for a limited number of gliders to have landed in the vicinity of the Bridge. Despite the flak, it might have paid us to have accepted even quite heavy casualties in order to get men south of the Bridge. It would have been cheaper in the long run.

The handicap of the division being landed in three lifts was one from which we never recovered. While I am quite certain that Browning could not have done better for us in the circumstances that faced him, the delay in developing the full strength of the division was serious. An airborne division is designed to fight as a whole and should be dropped or landed as such. The corps' plan was intended to make certain of the objectives in the order of their importance, which was from bottom to top. Yet the effect of this was that our task, for which four brigade groups were allocated, was tackled on the first and vital day by only one – the 1st Parachute Brigade.

The others on the first day were defending the dropping zones. Even with the protection we provided, the 4th Parachute Brigade's landings were contested, and the opposition would have been accentuated if the KOSB and the Border Regiment had not been present to safeguard the arrival. If alternative dropping zones had been available for the second and third lifts, it would have paid us to use them in order to maintain the surprise and free the covering force. As things turned out, the troops used in the protection of the DZs and LZs would have been invaluable offensively during the first twenty-four hours. Perhaps our ideas were wrong.

There is no doubt that we came off badly in the street fighting. Most of us had not taken this problem specifically into account when the plan was made or even during the move into the town. All eyes and thoughts were on the Bridge. Although everyone had done some training in street fighting, not enough thought had been given to the obstacles produced in a built-up area where free movement was so hampered. When troops were fired upon during the move into town they tended to gravitate to the nearest ditch or to take cover where they could, and if the firing was prolonged they got into the closest houses and stayed there as long as there was opposition. The high garden walls and wire fences made movement off the roads a laborious business, and we failed to make enough use of the side roads also because nobody knew where they led and we were short of town maps. We would have made more headway if we had used the civilian's local knowledge to a greater extent, and if we had taken more advantage of the Dutch liaison officers attached to the division.

We should have taken more short cuts.

Our main preoccupation was to push along the main roads, and there were not many of these. As soon as opposition built up on these roads, we were halted. A built-up area is hell for the attacker and an asset to those in defence, as we discovered ourselves during the later stages of the battle.

In the early stages, most of us tended to think that the opposition was not more than passing and that sooner or later we would get on. Yet even the restricted movement produced by the Arnhem road system and our failure to use the secondary roads adequately would not have prevented a switch of some units – *if* our wireless communications had worked better. Certainly the 3rd Battalion could have been switched to the lower road earlier to follow the 2nd Battalion which reached the Bridge. As it turned out, the presence of the 1st, 3rd and 11th Parachute Battalions and the South Staffords in the same built-up area was chaotic. Near Den Brink, where the opposition became hottest, the steepness of the ground down to the riverside off the main road and the difficulty of moving among the houses near the Museum on the other side produced a bottleneck and terrible confusion. Company and platoon commanders were separated, the wireless failed, and there was a lack of firm control and local tactical planning.

Yet it was unbelievable that the conditions were such that the best part of four battalions should cease to exist. It was not due to lack of morale or training.

It is problematical whether two or even three battalions would have been enough at the Bridge. Frost and his small force did wonderfully to have lasted as long as they did, and in the way they fought. Obviously with additional units our defence would have been stronger and might have lasted longer. I doubt however, in view of the opposition and the time taken by XXX Corps, whether anything less than the whole division, plus the Polish Brigade, would have been able to hold the Bridge area until the arrival of the 2nd Army. We still would not have been able to prevent a certain amount of German movement towards Nijmegen from the Reichwald Forest.

I have often thought that my own movements in the first few days of the battle are open to criticism. Normally at the start of a battle there is little that a commander can do to influence affairs except to see for himself what is taking place. Often his very presence can be an encouragement to the troops and sometimes he can ginger up individuals or units who are not moving as quickly as they should. I did not visualize any major decision being required from me during the early stages – if the landings went well, which they did – but I thought that later it might be very difficult for me to get about because the battle would have been seriously joined and I would be busy. I hardly expected that I would be pinned to the ground and forced for some thirty-six hours to move with one of the battalions into a state of inactivity. It might have been better if I had stayed with my HQ, even though I had little to do at the start. I would certainly then have been able to take more of a grip on the subsequent actions of the Airlanding Brigade and the 4th Parachute Brigade, and I would have spared two brigadiers some unpleasantness.

Yet it is against one's nature and training just to hang about at HQ. In nine cases out of ten, I am sure, a commander should get out and about once he is satisfied that the plan he has made is sound and that it has been satisfactorily launched. Sooner or later I *would* have gone up to the 1st Parachute Brigade to see how it was getting on and to meet Lathbury. The only difference might have been in the timing. But with the failure of communications which bedevilled us from the start, it was even more necessary for me to visit the commanders of the formations.

There were many other factors which contributed to the end result at Arnhem.

The speed and efficiency of the German reaction was impressive: the German soldier has always been trained in immediate counter-attack and this was shown in the early days at Arnhem. The junior leadership was good, and the ability and willingness of the German soldier, whatever his medical category, to take some action was marked. The gallantry of individual snipers was commendable.

The lack of close air support was a surprise to us. In the first two or three days before the flak started to build up, low-flying rocket aircraft would have been invaluable. Little was to be seen of the Luftwaffe, and rooftop attacks by Allied fighters on tanks in the streets would have made a lot of difference. The targets would have been hard to pinpoint and much would have depended on the individual pilot and his ability to stooge around for a while free from enemy interference. This condition could not, of course, be guaranteed, and in view of the exaggerated intelligence picture concerning flak, could hardly have been attempted. Whatever the reasons, fighter support was not forthcoming except in small numbers and very late in the battle.

Much has been made since the war of a tale that we were betrayed by a Dutch Underground leader, Christian Lindemans, otherwise known as 'King Kong' for his tremendous bulk and feats of physical strength. He tipped off the Germans about 'Market Garden' and thereby caused the Hohenstaufen SS Panzer Division to be ready for us – or so the story goes. In fact, it has been established that Lindemans knew nothing about the operation, though he was certainly an informer for the Gestapo.

He took on the double duties after one of his younger brothers had been caught by the Gestapo in Underground work. In exchange for assurances about his brother's fate, Lindemans proceeded to give away his colleagues to the Germans. Any suspicions the partisans felt about him were dispelled when he was hit in the chest by a stray German bullet. Lindemans kept up his double game.

On Friday September 15th, two days before our operations in Holland, he called on the German counter-espionage organization and told an Abwehr major named Kiesewetter that the Allies were preparing a big attack in which they intended to take Eindhoven and then roll northwards. Lindemans produced a copy of the instructions to the Underground at Eindhoven warning them to be ready for September 17th. As the British and Canadians were already moving on a northerly axis, and would presumably not stop at Eindhoven, Kiesewetter and his chief, Colonel Giskes, attached no importance to the information. Lindemans did not mention Arnhem.

He was arrested at the end of the war, but committed suicide in prison the day before his trial was due to open in Holland. I have since talked to German officers who were at Arnhem, and who were taken completely by surprise when we landed. A retired Dutch Army officer, Lieutenant-Colonel Boeree, has gone to some trouble since the war to produce detailed evidence which to my mind establishes beyond doubt that Lindemans had no influence on the fate of my division. Perhaps the most convincing single demonstration of German unawareness was Field-Marshal Model's narrow escape from capture soon after the landings. And the proximity of the Hohenstaufen Division was purely coincidental.

Even when one has taken into account every possible set-back, large and small, which occurred during our nine days north of the Neder Rhine, the fact remains that we were alone for much longer than any airborne division is designed to stay. I think it is possible that for once Horrocks's enthusiasm was not transmitted adequately to those who served under him, and it may be that some of his more junior officers and NCOs did not fully comprehend the problem and the importance of great speed. By and large, the impression is that they were 'victory happy'. They had advanced north-wards very fast and had been well received by the liberated peoples, and they were not out of touch with the atmosphere of bullets and the battle. As is always the case, it took them a little time to attune themselves once more to the stern reality of tough fighting against the Germans. At first, the opposition seems to have caused them a certain amount of shock and surprise.

Nevertheless, the gallantry of the Guards Armoured Division at Nijmegen was marked, and I shall never cease to admire the excellent efforts of the 82nd US Airborne Division and in particular the combat team which brought off the fine river crossing at Nijmegen. The armoured-cars of the Household Cavalry did well, too, to get up to the banks of the Neder Rhine, and I have often wondered why the route they took could not have been followed immediately by other troops of XXX Corps. Once the Nijmegen Bridge was crossed, it would have been possible to send an armoured group along the Household Cavalry route followed by the infantry of the 43rd Division. It appears, however, that too much reliance was placed on armour and on the main axis. Once the tanks had come to a halt on the narrow roads built up above the polder between Nijmegen and Arnhem, they could not be manœuvred. Even with the main road through Elst blocked, which made it impossible for XXX Corps to reach the Arnhem Bridge, it might still have been practical for a fairly strong force to reach the bank south of our perimeter and to be ferried across. In the earlier stages, it might even have been possible to put a floating bridge across the river and thus enable us to extend the perimeter with a view to a further advance when the force had been sufficiently built up.

When the 43rd Division arrived, however, it was too late.

Horrocks remained optimistic to the very last about the possibility of effecting a crossing to the west of the perimeter. In this, I think he was being unrealistic; it is as well that Browning and Dempsey insisted that we came out when we did.

In my official report of the battle in January 1945 I wound up by saying:

> The operation was not one hundred per cent successful and did not end quite as we intended.
>
> The losses were heavy but all ranks appreciate that the risks involved were reasonable. There is no doubt that all would willingly undertake another operation under similar conditions in the future.
>
> We have no regrets.

I hold the same view today, when the survivors are scattered all over the world, some of them still in the Army; when Arnhem is a busy and architecturally attractive post-war city with most of its scars healed. A new bridge spans the Neder Rhine. Sometimes a Dutchman finds a mortar splinter in his garden, and people on their Sunday walks come across spent British ammunition in the pine woods and the polder-land by the river.

# APPENDIXES

## I

*Top Secret*

### OPERATION 'MARKET'

#### INSTRUCTION No 1

To: Major-General R. E. Urquhart, DSO
Commander 1 British Airborne Division,
with 1 Polish Parachute Brigade under
Command.

### 1. PRIMARY TASK

Your Primary task is to capture the ARNHEM bridges or a bridge.

### 2. SECONDARY TASK

Your Secondary task is to establish a sufficient bridgehead to enable the follow-up formations of 30 Corps to deploy NORTH of the NEDER RIJN.

### 3. THIRD TASK

During your operations immediately after the landing of the first lift, you will do all in your power to destroy the flak in the area of your DZs, LZs and ARNHEM to ensure the passage of your subsequent lifts.

### 4. JUNCTION POINTS

(*a*) In order to preserve your southern bomb line, no attempt will be made to effect a junction with 82 US Airborne Division to the SOUTH.

(*b*) At the southernmost point you hold on the main axis of 30 Corps, whether NORTH or SOUTH of the NEDER RIJN, you will establish a liaison party who will organize the reception and pass through of the follow-up formations (most probably the Guards Armoured Division; this, however, will be confirmed when known for certain).

This liaison party will have full information of the enemy dispositions, your own, routes open, etc. The rank of the officer in charge of the liaison party will be Lieut-Col or above.

The time at which you are to expect junction with 30 Corps leading troops will be notified to you from Corps Headquarters as soon as it is definitely known. This information may not be available to you until some time after you have landed.

## 5. 30 CORPS PLAN

30 Corps plan will be made available to you by, at the latest, Friday evening 15 September.

## 6. ENEMY INFORMATION

The latest Intelligence will be sent to you up to the time of take-off.

| | |
|---|---|
| HQ Airborne Troops (Main) | (Sgd) F. A. M. BROWNING. |
| c/o APO ENGLAND. | Lieutenant General. |
| 13 Sep 44. | Commander British Airborne Corps. |

# II

*NOT to be taken into the air.*        *TOP SECRET*
*Date: 12 Sep 44.*

OPERATION 'MARKET'      *Copy No. ....*

1 AIRBORNE DIV OP INSTR NO 9

CONFIRMATORY NOTES ON GOCS VERBAL ORDERS

Ref Maps: 1/25000 GSGS 4427, GINKEL 388, EDE 387, RENEN 5 NE, ARNHEM 6 NW

     1/100000 GSGS 2541 Sheets 2 and 5.
         „   4416 Sheet P.1

INFM
   1. (a) Issued verbally.
      (b) 1 Polish Para Bde Gp is under comd.

2. 1 Airborne Div will seize ARNHEM 7378 and the crossings over the NEDER RIJN and est a bridgehead to the NORTH of that town.

### METHOD

3. *Aircraft Allotment.*
  As for Op 'LINNET' – practically Scale 'Y'

4. The Div will land in three lifts

| | |
|---|---|
| *(a) First Lift.* | Tac Div HQ |
| | 1 Airlanding Recce Sqn |
| | 1 Lt Regt (Less one Bty) |
| | 1 Para Bde |
| | 1 A tk Bty RA |
| | 1 Para Sqn RE |
| | 16 Para Fd Amb |
| | 1 Airlanding Bde (Less certain sub units) |
| | 9 Fd Coy RE |
| | 181 Airlanding Fd Amb |
| *(b) Second Lift.* | 4 Para Bde |
| | 4 Para Sqn RE |
| | 133 Para Fd Amb |
| | 2 A tk Bty RA |

One Bty Lt Regt

Balance Div Glider Element

Balance 1 Airlanding Bde

Re-supply

| | |
|---|---|
| *(c) Third Lift.* | 1 Polish Para Bde Gp (Less Lt Bty) |

5. *Tasks*

#### First Lift

1 *Para Bde* with under comd  1 A tk Bty
                              1 Para Sqn RE
                              Dets 9 Fd Coy RE
                              16 Para Fd Amb
                              Recce Sqn (Less one tp)
          DZ 'X'                    LZ 'Z'

will (*a*) Seize and hold ARNHEM in order of priority
        (i) Main br at 746768
       (ii) Pontoon br at 738774

  (*b*) On arrival of second lift, seize and occupy sector allotted.

  (*c*) Occupy part of 1 Polish Para Bde sector until it arrives with third lift.

  (*d*) Cover DZ 'K' during the drop of 1 Polish Para Bde.

  (*e*) After Div sector has been occupied, make one bn available at short notice for Div res.

6. 1 *Airlanding Bde* with under comd 181 Airlanding Fd Amb
                  LZ 'S'

will (*a*) Secure LZs 'S' and 'Z'
         DZ 'X'
        and cover unloading of first lift.

  (*b*) Est posts at
       (i) Rd EDE 5785 – ARNHEM in vicinity of PLANKEN WAMBUIS 6683.
      (ii) Rd WAGENINGEN 5876 – ARNHEM in vicinity of RENKUM 6276.

  (*c*) Protect the arrival of the second lift
     on DZs 'Y' and 'X'
     LZs 'S' and 'Z'

  (*d*) After unloading of second lift has been completed, seize and occupy the sector allotted.

  (*e*) Protect landing of Polish gliders in third lift on LZ 'L'.

7. *Recce Sqn*
  (*a*) Less one tp will come under comd 1 Para Bde for seizure of brs at ARNHEM. Dets 9 Fd Coy will be under comd.

  (*b*) One tp of Div res to RV HALTE WOLFHESEN 665805.

  (*c*) On completion task with 1 Para Bde will revert to Div and RV HEIJONOORD 725785. Dets 9 Fd Coy revert CRE.

  (*d*) Div tasks – recce in priority –

| rd APELDORN | 7803 – ARNHEM |
| ,, ZUTPEN | 9494 – ,, |
| ,, ZEVENAR | 8571 – ,, |
| ,, NIJMEGEN | 7062 – ,, |
| ,, WAGENINGEN | 5876 – ,, |
| EDE | 5785 |

8. 21 *Indep Para Coy*

will mark

|  |  |  |  |
|--|--|--|--|
| DZs | 'X' | 'Y' | 'K' |
| LZs | 'S' | 'Z' | 'L' |
| SDP | 'V' | | |

for first, second and third lifts.

On completion task will RV DER BRINK 718779.

9. *RA*

 (a) (i) Lt Regt less one bty under comd CRA.
 3 Lt Bty in sp 1 Para Bde.
 1 Lt Bty in sp 1 Airlanding Bde.

 (ii) Initial gun area 6779 – 3 Bty moving to 6977.

 (iii) FOOs as detailed by CRA.

 (b) *A tk*

 (i) 1 A tk Bty (less one 17-pr tp) under comd 1 Para Bde.

 (ii) One 17-pr tp for protection of Div tps.

10. *RE*

 (a) 1 *Para Sqn RE*
 On arrival second lift, 1 Para Sqn (less one tp remaining under comd 1 Para Bde) reverts to under comd CRE. Sqn RV POWER STATION 753768.

 (b) 9 *Fd Coy RE and det 261 Fd Pk Coy RE*
 (i) 2 dets 9 Fd Coy under comd Recce Sqn.
 Task to neutralize and remove charges on brs.
 On arrival second lift, dets revert to under comd 9 Fd Coy RV TAFELLAAN 717792.

 (ii) One *tp* 9 *Fd Coy* under comd 1 Airlanding Bde from time of arrival LZ.

 (iii) 9 *Fd Coy RE* (less one tp and dets) and *det* 261 *Fd Pk Coy* under comd CRE. RV TAFELLAAN 717792.

11. *Tac Div*

Lands on LZ 'Z'. RV track junc 657797, thence main rd WAGENINGEN–ARNHEM. Opens ARTILLERIE PARK 7378.

|              Tasks              |       Second Lift       |
| ------------------------------- | ----------------------- |
| 12. 4 *Para Bde* with under comd | 4 Para Sqn RE          |
|                                 | 133 Para Fd Amb         |
|                                 | 2 A tk Bty RA           |
| DZ 'Y'                          | LZ 'X'                  |

will (*a*) Seize and occupy sector allotted.

Axis of movement rd EDE – ARNHEM.

(*b*) Occupy part of sector alloted to 1 Polish Para Bde until its arrival with third lift.

13. *RA*

(*a*) *Arty*

(i) 2 Lt Bty in sp 4 Para Bde.

(ii) Gun area for Lt Regt in main posn 7177.

(*b*) *A tk*

(i) 1 A tk Bty reverts under comd CRA and in sp 1 Para Bde

(ii) 2 A tk Bty (less one 17-pr tp) in sp 4 Para Bde.

(iii) Two 17-pr tps and one 6-pr tp in Div res under CRA.

14. *RE*

4 *Para Sqn RE*

On arrival third lift, 4 Para Sqn RE (less one tp remaining under comd 4 Para Bde) reverts to under comd CRE.

RV ARNHEM rly stn 732782.

15. *Re-supply*

35 Stirlings on LZ 'L'.

Principal contents gun amn and mortar bombs. Some pet.

|           Tasks           |    Third Lift    |
| ------------------------- | ---------------- |
| 16. 1 *Polish Para Bde Gp* |                 |
| DZ 'K'                    | LZ 'L'           |

will occupy sector allotted with a minimum of delay.

17. *Re-supply*

100 aircraft plus DZ 'V'.

18. *Method of occupation*

Bdes will put out false front and standing patrols as far as is practicable. No attempt at co-ordination by Div will be made until arrival on ground and resources and situation are known.

19. *Bomb Line*
  (a) *As from H hr until second lift + 6 hrs*
    785855 – 768852 – 750846 – 737845 – 730844 – 715845 – 708851 – 695852 – 676853 – 659853 – 639853 – 628853 – 613855.
  (b) *As from second lift + 6 hrs (i.e. not before 11 00 hrs D + 1)*
    629852 – 629842 – 630821 – 628807 – 623788 – 616772 – 614759.
  (c) Bde Comds will submit targets on which they wish pre-briefed bombing either before or after H hr.


20. *Glider Pilots*
Will remain with units landed until Div sector has been occupied.
Then: One bn remains under comd 1 Airlanding Bde.
  One bn in Div res RV SONSBEEK 743785.


21. *Timings*
  (a) *First Lift*
      H hr (main glider lift starts landing) approx 14 00 hrs.
      D-day, but not before 10 00 hrs.
  (b) *Second and Third Lifts*
      As early as possible on D + 1 and D + 2.


22. *Briefing*
No briefing below unit comds and heads of services without further instrs from Div HQ.


23. *Recognition Signs*
  (a) Ground to air: yellow smoke or flares, and yellow fluorescent panels, if available.
  (b) Ground to ground: yellow celanese triangles.


24. *Passwords*

| | Challenge | RED |
| --- | --- | --- |
| H hr until 23 59 hrs D-day | | |
| | Reply | BERET |
| 23 59 hrs D-day until 23 59 hrs D + 1 | Challenge | UNCLE |
| | Reply | SAM |
| 23 59 hrs D + 1 until 23 59 hrs D + 2 | Challenge | CARRIER |
| | Reply | PIGEON |
| 23 59 hrs D + 2 until 23 59 hrs D + 3 | Challenge | AIR |
| | Reply | BORNE |

|  | | | |
|---|---|---|---|
| 23 59 hrs D + 3 until 23 59 hrs D + 4 | Challenge | ROBERT | |
| | Reply | BURNS | |
| 23 59 hrs D + 4 until 23 59 hrs D + 5 | Challenge | TROOP | |
| | Reply | CARRIER | |

*ADM*

25. Issued separately.


26. Col H. N. BARLOW, Deputy Comd 1 Airlanding Bde, is appointed Town Commandant, ARNHEM. He will maintain close touch with Comd 1 Para Bde and will co-ordinate the tasks of the APM and OC Fd Security Sec.

*INTERCOMN*

27. Sigs instrs issued separately.


28. Only 30 Corps list of code names for places, as issued for COMET, will be used. Fmns and units may, however, give code names to important routes, axis of advance, or detailed objectives, at their discretion.

*ACK*

| | | |
|---|---|---|
| Time of Signature | 15 30 hrs. | Lt-Col GS, |
| Method of Despatch | By hand. | 1 Airborne Division. |


*TACK HQ*

### Distribution

| | Copy No. | | Copy No. |
|---|---|---|---|
| 1 Para Bde | 1 | RASC | 17 |
| 4 Para Bde | 2 | Med | 18 |
| 1 Airlanding Bde | 3 | APM | 19 |
| Recce Sqn | 4 | ORD | 20 |
| RA | 5 | Reme | 21 |
| RE | 6 | Pro | 22 |
| Sigs | 7 | HQ Airtps (6) | 23–28 |
| 21 Indep Para Coy | 8 | 52 (L) Div | 29 |
| 1 Polish Para Bde | 9 | 82 US Airborne Div | 30 |
| GOC | 10 | 101 US Airborne Div | 31 |
| G (Ops) | 11 | Comd Glider Pilots (3) | 32–34 |
| 1 Airborne Div (Main) (2) | 12–13 | GSO1 (Air) IX TCC | 35 |
| G (Air) | 14 | GSO1 (Air) 38 Gp RAF | 36 |
| G (Int) | 15 | War Diary (2) | 37–38 |
| AQ | 16 | File | 39 |
| | | Spares | 40–50 |

# III

## 'MARKET'

### GLIDER ALLOTMENT BY LIFTS

| Unit | 1st Lift | 2nd Lift | 3rd Lift |
|---|---|---|---|
| Div HQ | 10 | 19 | |
| Recce Sqn | 22 | — | |
| Lt Regt | 57 | 33 | |
| 1 A Tk Bty | 21 | — | |
| 2 A Tk Bty | — | 27 | |
| 17 Pr Bty | 11<br>(incl 8 Hamilcars) | 11<br>(incl 8 Hamilcars) | |
| 9 Fd Coy RE | 16 | 6 | |
| 1 Para Bde | 23<br>(incl 3 Hamilcars) | 20 | |
| 4 Para Bde | — | 43<br>(incl 3 Hamilcars) | |
| HQ 1 A/L Bde | 10<br>(incl 1 for Pro) | — | |
| Airlanding Bn | 57<br>(incl 1 Hamilcar) | 6 | |
| Airlanding Bn | 57<br>(incl 1 Hamilcar) | 6 | |
| Airlanding Bn | 22 | 41<br>(incl 1 Hamilcar) | |
| 181 A/L Fd Amb | 7 | 5 | |
| 21 Indep Para Coy | — | 1 | |
| Adm | 7 | 36<br>(incl 3 Hamilcars) | |
| Polish Para Bde | — | 45 | 35 |
| Corps HQ | 38 | — | — |
| Unallotted | — | 2 | — |
| | 358 | 301 | 35 |

Total Glider Allotment: 694.

# IV

## OPERATION 'MARKET'
### Unit Allotment to Airfields

### A. PARACHUTE AIRCRAFT

**1st Lift. 1 Para Bde**

| Serial | Airfield | Bde HQ | 1 Bn | 2 Bn | 3 Bn | 1 Para Sqn RE | 16 (P) Fd Amb | Recce | 21 Indep Para Coy | 4 Bde Adv Pty | Div HQ | RASC | Total |
|---|---|---|---|---|---|---|---|---|---|---|---|---|---|
| 1 | FAIRFORD | | | | | | | | 12 | | | | 12 |
| 2 | FOLKINGHAM | | | 34 | 34 | | 4 | | | | | | 72 |
| 3 | BARKSTON HEATH | 9 | 34 | | | 9 | 2 | 8 | | 4 | 5 | 2 | 73 |
| | | | | | | | | | | | | | 157 |

**2nd Lift. 4 Para Bde** (sub-columns: Bde HQ | 156 Bn | 10 Bn | 11 Bn | 4 Para Sqn RE | 133 (P) Fd Amb | RASC)

| Serial | Airfield | Bde HQ | 156 Bn | 10 Bn | 11 Bn | 4 Para Sqn RE | 133 (P) Fd Amb | Recce | | 4 Bde Adv Pty | Div HQ | RASC | Total |
|---|---|---|---|---|---|---|---|---|---|---|---|---|---|
| 4 | SALTBY | | 33 | 33 | | | | 2 | | | 2 | | 70 |
| 5 | COTTESMORE | 8 | | | 33 | 9 | 4 | | | | | | 54 |
| | | | | | | | | | | | | | 124 |

**3rd Lift**

| Serial | Airfield | | Total |
|---|---|---|---|
| 6 | SPANHOE | 1 Polish Para Bde | 54 |
| 7 | COTTESMORE | 1 Polish Para Bde | 60 |
| | | | 114 |

Total Parachute Aircraft — 395

# V

## 1 AIRBORNE DIVISION ORDER OF BATTLE
## OPERATION 'MARKET'

**HQ 1** *Airborne Div*

| | |
|---|---|
| GOC | Major-General R. E. Urquhart DSO |
| ADC | Capt G. C. Roberts |
| GSO 1 (Ops) | Lt-Col C. B. Mackenzie |
| GSO 2 (Ops) | Major O. F. Newton-Dunn |
| GSO 2 (Air) | Major D. J. Madden |
| GSO 2 (Int) | Major H. P. Maguire |
| AA & QMG | Lt-Col P. H. H. H. Preston |
| DAAG | Major L. K. Hardman |
| DAQMG | Major E. R. Hodges |

HQ RA

| | |
|---|---|
| CRA | Lt-Col R. G. Loder-Symonds DSO |
| BMRA | Major P. T. Tower MBE |

HQ RE

| | |
|---|---|
| CRE | Lt-Col E. C. W. Myers CBE, DSO |
| Adjt RE | Capt M. D. Green |

Divisional Signals

| | |
|---|---|
| OC Div Sigs | Lt-Col T. C. V. Stephenson |
| 2 i/c | Major A. J. Deane-Drummond MC |

HQ RASC

| | |
|---|---|
| CRASC | Lt-Col M. St J. Packe |
| 2 i/c | Major D. G. Clark |

Medical Serivces

| | |
|---|---|
| ADMS | Col G. M. Warrack |
| DADMS | Major J. E. Miller MC |

RAOC

| | |
|---|---|
| ADOS | Lt-Col G. A. Mobbs |

**REME**
    Adj REME          Capt F. W. Ewens

**RAChD**
    SCF               Major A. W. H. Harlow

**Pro**
    APM              Major O. P. Haig

**1 *Para Bde***

| | |
|---|---|
| Comd | Brigadier G. W. Lathbury DSO MBE |
| BM | Major J. A. Hibbert |
| DAA & QMG | Major C. D. Byng-Maddick |
| 1 Para Bn | Lt-Col D. Dobie DSO |
| 2 Para Bn | Lt-Col J. D. Frost DSO, MC |
| 3 Para Bn | Lt-Col J. A. C. Fitch |
| Recce Sqn (less one tp) | Major C. F. H. Gough MC |
| 3 A/L Lt Bty RA | Major D. S. Mumford |
| 1 A/L A-Tk Bty RA | Major W. F. Arnold |
| 1 Para Sqn RE | Major D. C. Murray MC |
| 16 Para Fd Amb | Lt-Col E. Townsend MC |
| Det RASC | |

**4 *Para Bde***

| | |
|---|---|
| Comd | Brigadier J. W. Hackett DSO, MBE, MC |
| BM | Major C. W. B. Dawson |
| 156 Para Bn | Lt-Col Sir W. R. de B. des Voeux |
| 10 Para Bn | Lt-Col K. B. I. Smyth OBE |
| 11 Para Bn | Lt-Col G. H. Lea |
| 2 A/L Lt Bty RA | Major J. E. F. Linton |
| 2 A/L A-Tk Bty RA | Major A. F. Haynes |
| 4 Para Sqn RE | Major A. E. J. M. Perkins |
| 133 Para Fd Amb | Lt-Col W. C. Alford |
| Det RASC | |

**1 *Airlanding Bde***

| | |
|---|---|
| Comd | Brigadier P. H. W. Hicks DSO, MC |
| Deputy Comd | Col H. N. Barlow |
| BM | Major C. A. H. B. Blake |

| 1 Border | Lt-Col T. Hadden |
| 7 KOSB | Lt-Col R. Payton-Reid |
| 2 South Staffords | Lt-Col W. D. H. McCardie |
| 1 A/L Lt Bty RA | Major A. F. Norman-Walker |
| 181 Fd Amb | Lt-Col A. T. Marrable |
| Det RASC | |

*Div Tps*

| 1st Light Regt RA | Lt-Col W. F. K. Thompson MBE |
| No. 1 FOU | Major R. Wight-Boycott |
| 9 Fd Coy RE | Major J. C. Winchester |
| 21 Indep Para Coy | Major B. A. Wilson |
| 250 Lt Coy RASC | |
| 93 Coy RASC (det) | |
| Ord Fd Pks (det) | |
| REME Wksps (det) | |
| 89 Fd Security Sec | Capt J. E. Killick |
| Div Pro Coy | Capt W. R. Gray |
| No 1 Wing, GP Regt | Lt-Col I. A. Murray DSO |
| No. 2 Wing, GP Regt | Lt-Col J. W. Place |

*Seaborne Tail*[1]

| OC | Major R. D. Sellon (KOSB) |
| Div HQ | Capt The Hon J. B. Coventry |
| 1 Para Bde | Major J. A. Jessop |
| 4 Para Bde | Major J. C. H. Eyles |
| A/L Bde | Major W. E. Balmer |
| Recce Sqn | Capt R. J. Clark |
| RASC | Major J. R. Halls |
| Lt Regt | Capt A. J. A. Hanhart |

[1]The Seaborne Tail comprised approximately a thousand vehicles, which contained equipment and stores that could not be taken by air. It was planned that it should join up with the division so that it could continue in a ground role after a junction had been made with the 2nd Army.

# General War Series

# British Battles Series

**BATTLES OF THE '45**                   30p
Katherine Tomasson & Francis Buist
The story of the fiercely fought engagements
which took place between the Royalist army and
the Jacobites, led by Prince Charles Edward.
'History as it should be written . . . infinite
research and highly entertaining' – BOOKS AND
BOOKMEN

**THE SPANISH ARMADA**                   30p
Michael Lewis
'A brilliant, clear picture of the campaign' –
BRITISH BOOK NEWS

**TRAFALGAR**                            30p
Oliver Warner
A stirring picture of the battle in which Nelson
died destroying Napoleon's power at sea.

**BATTLES OF THE ENGLISH CIVIL
        WAR**                            30p
Austin Woolrych
'An excellent book. Covers the three decisive
engagements which sealed the fate of King
Charles I; Marston Moor which lost him the
North, Naseby which lost him most of his army
and Preston which lost him his head' – DAILY
TELEGRAPH

**THE BATTLE OF THE ATLANTIC** 30p
Donald Macintyre
Extracts of the logbooks of both warship and
U-boat commanders help tell the gripping
story of those crucial months from 3rd September, 1939 to 24th May, 1943. 'A story which
must never be forgotten' – THE NAVY

# *Battle of Britain Series*